ORIGINAL SIGNS

ORIGINAL
SIGNS

Gesture, Sign,
and the Sources
of Language

David F. Armstrong

Gallaudet University Press | *Washington, D.C.*

Gallaudet University Press
Washington, DC 20002

Library of Congress Cataloging-in-Publication Data

Armstrong, David F.
    Original signs : gesture, sign, and the sources of language /
    David F. Armstrong.
        p.   cm.
    Includes bibliographical references and index.
    ISBN 1-56368-075-0 (alk. paper)
    1. Language and languages—Origin.   2. Sign language.   3. Gesture.
I. Title.
P116.A754   1999
401—dc21   98-49671
                                                                    CIP

And when the woman saw that the tree was good for food, and that it was pleasant to the eyes, and a tree to be desired to make one wise, she took of the fruit thereof, and did eat, and gave also unto her husband with her; and he did eat.

Genesis 3.6

Contents

Acknowledgments

THE AUTHOR WISHES to express his gratitude to the following individuals who read and commented on various drafts of this book: Sherman Wilcox, Stuart Shanker, Barbara King, and two anonymous reviewers for Gallaudet University Press. Robert C. Johnson and Michael Shirley of Gallaudet University generously provided drawings and graphics. Ivey Pittle Wallace and Vic Van Cleve of Gallaudet University Press gave very helpful guidance throughout the preparation of the manuscript. My deepest appreciation is reserved for William C. Stokoe. Without his genius and generosity this book could not have been written.

Introduction: The Forest of Symbols

IT IS COMMON for human beings to think of their bodies, their languages, and their minds either as special creations of a supernatural agency or as the ultimate end products of a purpose-driven or teleological evolutionary process. This book will not deal with the first of these beliefs, in that it has a purpose different from but not necessarily at odds with religious explanation. It will, instead, attempt to provide an alternative to the second belief, with respect to the origin of language. In pursuit of this goal, it will take an explicitly Darwinian perspective on the origin and evolution of the human capacity for language and abstract thought. In this context, the term *Darwinian* should be taken to imply that evolution of all the earth's organisms is fundamentally undirected, involving the creation of new traits through random mutations of the genetic material (see fig. 1). This does not mean that anything is possible—limitations are certainly imposed on the directions of later evolutionary paths by earlier occurrences. In this sense, evolutionary change may be said to be "channeled." One example of this that will be discussed in greater detail in chapter 1 is that of human bipedalism, an unusual form of locomotion that may have been made possible by an earlier locomotor adaptation of apes. However, the Darwinian perspective implies that at no point was the evolution of bipedalism predictable or inevitable.

The most basic assumption of such a perspective is that the current outcomes of such processes are not predictable from knowledge, no matter how detailed, of initial conditions. Many rational people consider this sort of indeterminacy to be emotionally and philosophically unacceptable, and the usual alternative is to pro-

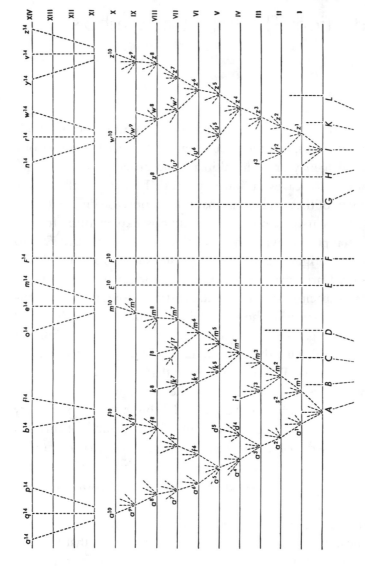

Fig. I. Darwin's original use of a tree diagram to represent the divergence of biological species. "The probable effects of the action of natural selection through divergence and extinction, on the descendants of a common ancestor." Reprinted from Darwin, *Origin of Species*, 115.

pose that evolution is teleological—that is, directed by some ultimate purpose or toward some predetermined design. For example, Father Pierre Teilhard de Chardin, a French priest and paleoanthropologist, proposed a teleological evolutionary alternative to Darwin in *The Phenomenon of Man.*[1] According to Teilhard de Chardin's formulation, human evolution could be seen as a sequence of steps toward ever more perfect forms.

To this need for certainty, Darwin had what may still be the most eloquent reply:

> When we no longer look at an organic being as a savage looks at a ship, as something wholly beyond his comprehension; when we regard every production of nature as one which has had a long history; when we contemplate every complex structure and instinct as the summing up of many contrivances, each useful to the possessor, in the same way as any great mechanical invention is the summing up of the labor, the experience, the reason, and even the blunders of numerous workmen; when we thus view each organic being, how far more interesting, I speak from experience, does the study of natural history become![2]

Darwin went on to write that "there is grandeur in this view of life" as a historical process, rather than an unfolding of predetermined structure, "with its several powers, having been originally breathed by the creator into a few forms or into one; and that, whilst this planet has gone cycling on according to the fixed law of gravity, from so simple a beginning endless forms most beautiful and most wonderful have been, and are being evolved."[3]

Many consider language to be the crowning achievement of human evolution, perhaps the one ability that defines our humanity more than any other. The central dogma of modern biology is that no characteristic of a living organism can be adequately understood in the absence of an understanding of its evolutionary history. If we are to take the Darwinian position seriously, then we must look for the origins of language and, hence, the key to understanding its essential characteristics in the history of our species. In that spirit, this book will attempt to follow a set of principles set forth in the first chapter—principles derived mainly from evolutionary biology. It will also address a series of questions that deviate somewhat from those usually posed by linguists. In this regard, it is necessary to acknowledge that standard linguistics, with some exceptions, suggests that the development of the individual, or ontogeny, and the development of the species, or phylogeny, are both teleological with respect to language.[4] These ideas, in turn, are derived from the notions that languages are best viewed as closed, formal systems, and that everything that is linguistically important can be expressed through speech.

Two major assumptions underlying the arguments in this book are derived from the author's personal experiences. It is significant that the author of this book, although a hearing person, has spent a large part of his adult life working and communicating with people who are deaf. He is personally acquainted with most of the people mentioned herein who have worked at understanding the nature of signed language, and numbers several of them among his closest friends. This has necessarily colored his perspective on several important issues concerning the scope of language as a biological phenomenon and its evolutionary history. Most important, from the perspective of readers of this book, is his conviction that language has always been a "multichannel" phenomenon. This is to say that for most people, most of the time, linguistic communication involves visible as well as vocal signs. This is the first of two principal assumptions underlying many of the arguments that will be presented herein, and there are, of course, notable exceptions to this generalization. For example, for people who are profoundly deaf, linguistic communication will necessarily be restricted almost exclusively to the visual channel. The second major assumption follows from the foregoing observations— people have always switched easily to signed languages when silence was obligatory. However, the assumption that language occupies a single channel, or that language is speech, is a misconception that underlies much of the speculation concerning the origins of language. This book represents an attempt to see what light can be shed on the subject when the approach taken is that language is inherently a multichannel, but primarily dual-channel activity, the two channels being the auditory and the visual.

Linguists commonly maintain that language is a system for translating the hierarchically organized contents of the mind into linear strings of arbitrary symbols. While this may (or may not) be an appropriate way to characterize speech, it is clearly not an appropriate way to characterize signed languages. The notion that language employs only a single channel has been carried over into the study of signed languages, and this is a misconception that may have been aided by the direct transfer of linguistic methods to the study of signed languages. By maintaining these positions, linguists have boxed themselves into a position from which it becomes extremely difficult to imagine how language (or the biological capacity for language) might have evolved according to the same processes as other biological systems. This book will suggest a different approach to understanding this process of evolution that takes into account the full range of human communicative behavior, by employing a more expansive notion of language. In this book, no strict separation will be made between language and human communication generally. That is, no strict separation will be made between language and gesture. In this view, human communication will be considered all-inclusive.

One could argue that the position taken here is wrongheaded in that the true field of study for linguistics is limited to speech, that what needs to be explained is speech and speech alone. Arguments will be presented here that this position is no longer tenable and needs a complete overhaul. Indeed, each of the assertions of traditional linguistics, presented above, are open to challenge. It is by now well known and generally accepted that when deaf people communicate using signed language, they are using a well-formed human language. However, the importance of this insight beyond the interests of the deaf community is not generally recognized. This simple observation should call attention to the fact that human beings regularly and habitually communicate linguistically using methods other than speech.

Stemming from the notion that languages are closed, formal systems is a corollary—that the best way to represent the data of linguistics is through tree diagrams. These diagrams, familiar from pedigree analysis and then from representations of the relationships among biological species, first appear in philology to represent the historical relationships among various languages.[5] The model is one of parent languages giving birth to daughters and sons that may then be subject to further reproduction with modification (see fig. 2). These diagrams have also been used to represent grammatical relationships among the elements of sentences and have appeared most recently in the syntactic theory of Chomsky[6] and other generative grammarians to represent the hierarchical relationships among the elements of phrases and sentences, in the manner of the data structures of the computing sciences. According to Steven Pinker, these tree structures constitute more than simply an attempt to represent grammatical relationships—they represent a theory about the way in which the brain actually does its linguistic computations.[7] Thus, anyone seriously considering the study of language today is confronted with a virtual forest of trees on which are hung the symbols of linguistics.

The tree, of course, is a particularly powerful symbol in Western culture and figures prominently in many of our myths and metaphors, so it is not surprising that it has come to occupy a central place in the study of language. The tree is, after all, a symbol of strength and renewable life, but above all it is a double-edged symbol of the sometimes arrogant, sometimes noble human quest for knowledge and wisdom. It is no accident that our central metaphor for scientific discovery is a falling apple striking Newton on the head, the fruit of the tree thereby imparting to him fundamental knowledge of the workings of the universe. A central theme of this book is that there are other, perhaps better, images than trees to picture the structures of individual languages

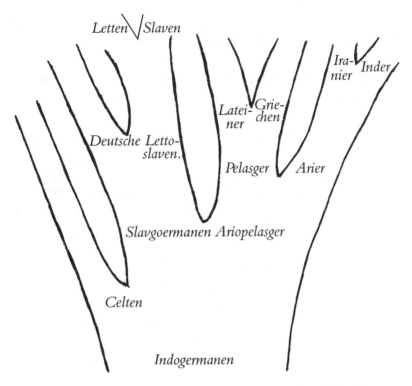

Letten\/*Slaven*

Ira- *Inder*
nier

Latei- *Grie-*
ner *chen*

Deutsche Letto-
slaven.

Pelasger *Arier*

Slavgoermanen Ariopelasger

Celten

Indogermanen

Fig. 2. Tree diagram of Indo-European languages, originally published in 1853. Redrawn from Otto von Schrader, *Sprachvergleichung und Urgeschichte: Linguistisch-historische Beiträge zur Erforschung des indogermanischen Altertums* (Jena: Hermann Costenoble, 1907), 56.

and the structures of interrelationship among all languages. Darwin's image of the "tangled bank" may be more apropos:

> It is interesting to contemplate a tangled bank, clothed with many plants of many kinds, with birds singing on the bushes, with various insects flitting about, and with worms crawling in the damp earth, and to reflect that these elaborately constructed forms, so different from each other, and dependent on each other in so complex a manner, have all been produced by laws acting around us.[8]

Though Darwin's views were sometimes ridiculed by his contemporaries (see fig. 3), his image provides a vehicle for viewing language as a complex of sequential, hierarchical processes, as well as processes that are more simultaneous and overlapping. It will also be argued that the interrelationships among the words or signs of a single language and the relationships among languages that contact one another are similarly complex and cannot be accounted for by the neatly branching trees of the linguist or logician.

Two very significant traditions in Western thought have had a profound impact on the development of linguistic theory. These traditions are descended from Plato and Descartes, respectively. In the Platonic scheme of the world, the ordinary manifestations of phenomena such as languages are thought of as pale and imperfect reflections of ideal forms, while the Cartesian program supports the notion of a mind–body dualism, in which the mind is governed by laws and forces other than those that govern the functions of the body. Throughout this book we will encounter treatments of language in which it is assumed that actual speech in a particular language is always an imperfect expression of a rigid, rule-based system, and that fundamental rules govern all languages. These latter rules, in turn, are said to be independent of other aspects of the cognitive or physiological functioning of human organisms. The Platonic and Cartesian tendencies in linguistics have thus led to the position that there are no significant differences among languages, other than surface variations in lexicon and syntax. This notion will be explored more fully herein, but it is worth noting that this was a progressive idea intended to counteract the racism and ethnocentrism of Western society. It may, however, have gone too far. This book takes seriously an older anthropological linguistics, propounded by the likes of Edward Sapir and Benjamin Lee Whorf, that asserted the worth of each language but that also considered each language as a natural experiment intimately connected to the culture of the people who spoke it.

An additional caveat is in order here. Few scholarly questions are more bound up in human politics than the major questions to be addressed in this book. The issues involved are central to ques-

PUNCH'S FANCY PORTRAITS.—NO. 54.

CHARLES ROBERT DARWIN, LL.D., F.R.S.

IN HIS *DESCENT OF MAN* HE BROUGHT HIS OWN SPECIES DOWN AS LOW
AS POSSIBLE—*I.E.*, TO "A HAIRY QUADRUPED FURNISHED WITH A TAIL
AND POINTED EARS, AND PROBABLY *ARBORRAL* IN ITS HABITS"—WHICH IS
A REASON FOR THE VERY GENERAL INTEREST IN A "FAMILY TREE." HE HAS
LATELY BEEN TURNING HIS ATTENTION TO THE "POLITIC WORM."

Fig. 3. Darwin's views were frequently ridiculed in the popular press during his lifetime. Reprinted from *Punch* 81 (22 October 1881): 190.

tions as fundamental as those surrounding the causes of the inequalities among current human populations. Increasing understanding is, therefore, dependent upon disentangling scientific and scholarly arguments from political ones—"deconstructing" these arguments, to use jargon that is current in some social science circles. In this regard, the author takes the dominant position resulting from the preponderance of anthropological research during the twentieth century—that no important behavioral differences among modern human populations can be ascribed to differences in gene frequencies. Besides being morally reprehensible, racist explanations of interpopulation differences in such things as social and technological complexity are also scientifically untenable. But this is emphatically not to say that no important differences among individuals are genetically based, nor is it to say that no important behavioral differences exist among human groups. Rather, the latter are better explained in terms of differences in ideology, in access to natural resources, or even in language than in characteristics of their gene pools.

The purpose of this book is not to present another "Just so story"[9] concerning the origin of language. However, it is maintained here that understanding language as a phenomenon entails understanding what is known about its origin and history. It is most important to understand that individual languages are human inventions. Because chimpanzees, our closest biological relatives, are apparently unable to construct or fully use human languages, we can conclude that the human ability to communicate through language must be based upon changes that have affected our genetic code since our ancestors separated from theirs. But this does not mean that, like Minerva springing fully armed from the brow of Jove,[10] individual languages spring fully formed from the brains, throats, or hands of human infants or adults. Languages must be learned over a lifetime, and they change and evolve over centuries. If, as Steven Pinker asserts, language is in some sense an instinct, then it is an instinct like no other in the animal kingdom.[11]

Pinker's assertion leads naturally to consideration of a fundamental philosophical and scientific issue—when we talk about the "origin and evolution" of language, exactly what is the topic of our discussion? Language is not a trait like eye color or stature, but an aspect of human behavior. The human ability to express and comprehend language and the kind of language that is used depend upon the presence and functioning of a variety of anatomical structures and physiological systems, including the senses of hearing and vision, the upper respiratory system, the hands and arms, and so on. Evolution occurs through changes in the frequencies of the genes that determine, through interaction with the environment, the functioning of such systems. Therefore, we must inevitably define not only language itself but also what is entailed by evolutionary change with respect to its expression. A recent debate between Pinker and the evolutionary biologist Stephen J. Gould reveals some of the most basic problems in this endeavor.[12]

On several occasions, Gould has criticized attempts to "explain" types of biological structure in terms of adaptation.[13] He has been particularly critical of the use of overly clever arguments to show genetic determination and a basis in natural selection for virtually every bizarre human custom. Against these arguments, Gould maintains that a variety of structures possessed by organisms are merely by-products of the presence of other structures, and that they are therefore not present because of the action of natural selection. He terms these "spandrels," after an architectural term for the space between two arches or the space between an arch and the rectangular framework surrounding it. Although the debate is quite general, it is easy to see that language might in some sense be such a spandrel—perhaps it is simply the by-product of an expanding brain and growing cognitive power. Pinker, on the other hand, takes the position that many human behavioral systems, including language, are "modular"—that is, they are analogous to independent, plug-in electronic components and under quite specific genetic control. Pinker also asserts that languages are adaptive in the sense of having evolved under natural selection.[14]

When two such obviously intelligent scholars disagree over matters this fundamental, the prudent student heads quickly for the middle ground. Neither metaphor, the spandrel nor the module, seems particularly apt when applied to language. By any reasonable standard, language clearly is more than a by-product of the evolution of other human traits—it is at the very center of human social activity, arguably the most basic human adaptation. The numerous anatomical and physiological systems currently emerging are best explained as products of coevolution with language. It should seem equally clear, however, that language is similarly not instinctive or modular—it involves a large number of physiological systems, and its processing and production involve much of the brain. Moreover, language shares certain features in common with other aspects of human behavior, and it shows considerable variation both among populations and historically.

At the outset of this book, it is necessary to draw the reader's attention to an issue of terminological usage. The word *sign* as used in this book generally refers to visible actions of people using what are usually called signed languages, for example, American Sign Language. However, at several points in the book the topic of discussion is the formal study of signs in a generic sense, or *semiotics*. In this sense, the word *sign* refers to elements of communication systems, and specifically, to things that stand for or indicate other things. In this sense, the words of spoken languages are signs, as are the signs of signed languages and several other classes of signifying activity such as pointing gestures. In general, the sense in which the word is being used should be clear from its context.

At the beginning of a book such as this, one is tempted to refer to Wittgenstein's apologia in the preface to his *Tractatus Logicophilosophicus*:

> If this work has any value, it consists in two things: the first is that thoughts are expressed in it, and on this score the better the thoughts are expressed—the more the nail has been hit on the

head—the greater will be its value.-Here I am conscious of having fallen a long way short of what is possible. Simply because my powers are too slight for the accomplishment of the task.-May others come and do it better.

On the other hand the *truth* of the thoughts that are here communicated seems to me unassailable and definitive. I therefore believe myself to have found, on all essential points, the final solution of the problems. And if I am not mistaken in this belief, then the second thing in which the value of this work consists is that it shows how little is achieved when these problems are solved.[15]

But this book has no pretensions either to his obscurity or to his profundity.

Notes

The title of the introduction is taken from the title of a book by Victor Turner (1967) and a poem by Baudelaire.

1. Teilhard de Chardin (1961).
2. Darwin ([1859] 1958, 447–48).
3. Ibid. (450).
4. See King and Shanker (1997).
5. For an interesting discussion of the history of tree diagrams in linguistics, see Stewart (1976). Stewart points out that tree diagrams appeared in philology before the publication of Darwin's *Origin* and seem to have come from prior representations of genealogies in this manner.
6. Chomsky (1965).
7. Pinker (1994).
8. Darwin ([1859] 1958, 450).
9. Theories of language origins are sometimes compared to the *Just so Stories* of Rudyard Kipling ([1902] 1992), fanciful children's stories about the origins of many things, including the leopard's spots and the alphabet.
10. See Hockett (1978).
11. Pinker (1994).
12. From an exchange of letters by Stephen J. Gould and Steven Pinker in the *New York Review of Books,* 1997.
13. For example, Gould and Lewontin (1979).
14. Pinker (1994).
15. Wittgenstein ([1921] 1974, 3–4).

1 | Where Did Language Come From?

HUMAN BEINGS HAVE long recognized the uniqueness of their ability to communicate through language and the importance of this ability to their success as a species. Attempts at explaining how it arose and diversified are also ancient. The biblical story of the Tower of Babel is well known, and there are other early accounts of the origin and diversification of language. With the advent of the Enlightenment in Europe, Western speculation about the origin of language became increasingly materialistic. One of the most influential of the Enlightenment writers to propose a gestural basis for language was the French savant, the Abbé de Condillac. Condillac believed that the first languages were gestural but that fully grammatical language presupposed the use of sound. According to Gordon Hewes, an anthropologist and historian of gestural-origin theories:

> In the mid-1740's, Condillac used to meet with Rousseau and Diderot for dinner in Paris, so that it is hardly strange that all three expressed ideas about glottogenesis [the origin of language]. Diderot, in his letter on the deaf and dumb (1751) observed that the natural order of ideas would be best revealed by studying the sign-language of the deaf. Although he set forth no language origin theory, he explained how a person deaf from birth might invent signs, such as for drinking, but that temporal relationships might be difficult to render gesturally.[1]

Ideas such as these were incorporated within an emerging Darwinian evolutionary framework in the late nineteenth century. At this point the arguments begin to become interesting from a modern scientific perspective. Even at this early stage of development, the arguments flow into two broad channels—one that tries to account for language in terms of continuity with a gestural precursor, and one that tries to account for language as uniquely a function of the vocal apparatus.

In fact, the idea that the first form of language might have been something like the signed languages of deaf people was a fairly common point of view in the period immediately following the publication of Darwin's *Origin of Species*. Following is an excerpt from Amos Kendall's introductory address at the inauguration of the College for the Deaf and Dumb (now Gallaudet University) in 1864. Kendall, a prominent politician and philanthropist (see fig. 4), had founded the school for the deaf that preceded the college at the same site in Washington:

> If the whole human family were destitute of the sense of hearing, they would yet be able to interchange ideas by signs. Indeed, the language of signs undoubtedly accompanied if it did not precede the language of sounds. Men are created, not with a God-given language, but with a God-given capacity to make signs and sounds, and by the use of these to form a language. No child comes into the world with a language; *that* is an *acquisition,* and the child always acquires the language of its parents, or of those by whom it is surrounded. It has ideas before it has a language in which to communicate them to others. Its only language is signs or incoherent cries. We read that Adam named the beasts and birds. But how could he give them names without first pointing them out by other means? How could a particular name be fixed upon a particular animal among so many species without some sign indicating to what animal it should thereafter be applied?[2]

Language, then, is a human acquisition in two senses. It is an acquisition made by each child who is raised in an even minimally acceptable environment, and it is an acquisition of the human species that has resulted during the course of our unique evolutionary history. Numerous theories concerning the nature of both processes of acquisition have been proposed. This book will be concerned with the acquisition of language in the latter sense—in terms of its evolutionary origins.

Fig. 4. Amos Kendall was a wealthy Washington philanthropist who donated the land that became Kendall Green, the home of Gallaudet College. Photograph courtesy of Gallaudet University Archives.

Theories of language origin can be divided into two general classes with respect to what has been called the issue of continuity. The first body of theory involves a gradualist orientation and hypothesizes that the biological capacity for language evolved slowly and incrementally within the ancestral lineage of modern human beings. This has been termed the "continuity hypothesis."

The second body of theory might be described in evolutionary terms as "saltational" or "punctuational," and it involves the assumption that the appearance of the capacity for language was relatively sudden—probably coincident with the appearance of anatomically modern *Homo sapiens*. This has been called the "discontinuity hypothesis." In general, modern arguments that have proposed a gestural or signing stage in language evolution have tended to fall in the continuity camp and have tended to see language as having quite ancient precursors.[3] However, many murky issues have surrounded these two general hypotheses in the debates, and not the least of these concerns the very nature of language itself. What is to be explained? Simply speech, or some more general capacity for language that could be expressed in a variety of modalities?

During the past three decades, an evolving body of literature describing the signed languages of deaf people has added a wholly new dimension both to speculation concerning the origin of language and to definitions of what constitutes language. The notion that these sign systems might be languages in the same sense as the world's spoken languages originated with William C. Stokoe, a language scholar who began working at Gallaudet University (then Gallaudet College) during the 1950s. Stokoe devised a descriptive system for what has come to be known as American Sign Language (ASL) that was based on the linguistic principle of contrast at the sublexical level (the level below the sign or word), thereby implying that signed languages might have identifiable "phonological" levels and greatly expanding the range of phenomena studied by linguists.[4] The concept of phonology as applied to signed languages will be explored much more fully in chapter 3, but it is sufficient here to know that a set of meaningless items that can be assembled to form meaningful words is considered a basic feature of language in many conceptions of linguistics.

Stokoe's work also buttressed reemerging attempts to describe the stages by which human languages emerged during the evolutionary history of the species, an area of inquiry that had fallen into disrepute. Speculation about the evolution of human languages intensified following the appearance of Darwin's *Origin of Species,* but with little supporting evidence, it tended to the outrageous. So much so, that in 1866 the Linguistic Society of Paris imposed a ban on such speculation at its meetings.[5] Stokoe and other anthropological and linguistic scholars, including Gordon Hewes and Charles Hockett, rescued this field of speculation during the 1960s and 1970s and put it on a sounder scientific footing.[6] In addition to work on signed languages, scientific knowledge was growing in other relevant areas, including the fossil record for human evolution and the behavior of our nearest biological relatives, the great apes of Africa and Asia.

Since Stokoe's initial insight, a large body of literature has arisen documenting attempts to define the extent of comparison that is possible between signed and spoken languages and the role that communication in each modality may have played in the evolution of the human capacity for language. Sherman Wilcox, a professor of linguistics and a teacher of ASL interpreters, has argued that much of this literature has had as its goal to show that the relationship in structure and underlying neurophysiology between signed and spoken languages is identity or near identity.[7] However, early in this endeavor Stokoe pointed out significant differences between signed and spoken languages resulting from differences in the capacities of the organs of perception sensitive to the visual and aural media.[8] In general, human beings have much greater sensory acuity in the visual medium, and this makes possible the use in signed languages of what semiotician Charles S. Peirce has termed "icons" to a degree impossible for spoken languages.

Following the two lines of thought just described, there have been two main approaches used to introduce sign language research into the language origins question. The first has been based on the assumption that signed languages and spoken languages have identical structural properties and in an evolutionary sense are substitutable one for another. In other words, signed languages would have little new to tell us about the evolution of language in general. The second approach assumes that because of their inherent "iconicity," signed languages might be similar, in some respects, to a gestural "prelanguage." It is not hard to see that the first approach would tend to be associated with discontinuity theories and the second with the continuity hypothesis. This should emphatically not be interpreted to mean that the signed languages of modern deaf people are in some way primitive, because they are not. With respect to the grammatical processes they employ, they are just as complex as modern spoken languages. The point that will emerge in this book, however, is that some of the devices that are employed by signed languages, such as iconicity, are plausible candidates for transitional devices in the evolution of language.

As we have seen, application of the results of modern scientific study of signed languages to the question of language origin began with papers by Gordon Hewes, William Stokoe, and the eminent American linguist, Charles Hockett. Broad-based theories deriving language from visible gesture were proposed. More recently, attempts have been made to apply gestural theory to specific problems in the origin and evolution of language—for example, the origins of syntax and duality of patterning or phonemicization. At the same time, scholars such as Derek Bickerton and Terrence Deacon have proposed that it is unnecessary to invoke a stage in the evolution of human language during which it was primarily signed or gestured.[9] This book will evaluate these positions from philosophical as well as biological perspectives, and it will be concerned primarily with what speculation about the origin of language can add to our understanding of the nature of the phenomenon itself.

Consideration of the recent debates that have surrounded the origin of language might lead some observers to conclude that there is a suspicious correlation between the theories and the scholarly specialties of the debaters. Many who have specialized in the linguistics of spoken languages see no role for signed languages in the emergence of language, and the obverse is true for those with a special interest in signing—the present author obviously belongs (quite unapologetically) to the latter camp. Derek Bickerton, a leading scholar of pidgins and creoles, sees a special role for these linguistic systems in the evolutionary process.[10] The position being promoted here is that no firm position is tenable in this debate. We simply cannot know with certainty what stages human beings may have passed through on their way to the development of modern languages. Because no direct evidence exists concerning the behavior of extinct human populations, these stages must be inferred. Therefore we should follow a set of principles based on the best available evidence. It is argued here that any theory concerning the origin of language and of its biological bases should

1. be directed at all of the forms that language has been known to take;
2. be based on empirical evidence;
3. not involve invented stages for which there is no precedent in either the fossil record or the known behavioral repertoires of the living primates;
4. be parsimonious;
5. invoke enhanced social communication as the primary selective force behind the evolution of language—human beings are the most social of the mammals, and our closest living relatives, chimpanzees, have social living as their primary adaptation, as well;
6. treat other potential driving forces, such as tool use and improved cognitive functioning, as secondary causes.

The arguments presented in this book may be considered to have succeeded to the extent that they follow these principles.

For the discussion that follows to make sense, it is necessary to introduce the reader, in very general terms, to what is currently known about the place that human beings occupy in the animal kingdom—especially about their genetic relationships with their closest living relatives. Human beings belong to the order Primates of the vertebrate class of mammals. The primates consist of two suborders: the Prosimii (including lemurs, galagos, and pottoes) and the Anthropoidea, which include monkeys, apes, and human beings. Within the Anthropoidea, human beings and the apes of Africa and Asia are grouped together in the superfamily Hominoidea. All of these subdivisions are made on the basis of presumed evolutionary relatedness, so this classification suggests that the closest relatives of human beings are the apes, including the gibbons and orangutans of Asia and the gorillas and chimpanzees of Africa. It is now known that, among the apes, gorillas and chimpanzees are most closely related to human beings, and, according to very recent studies of DNA among these three species, chimpanzees and human beings are probably more closely related to each other than either is to gorillas.[11] Indeed, at the level of the structure of DNA, the genetic material, chimpanzees and human beings are extremely similar with respect to its chemical sequences.

It is also important to know that several extinct species of human beings have been identified as having lived since the divergence of the lineages leading to modern human beings and modern chimpanzees. All of these fossil species, as well as modern human beings (*Homo sapiens*) are members of the family Hominidae, the hominids. All living human beings are member of the same species, *Homo sapiens,* which, in turn, is the only living representative of the Hominidae. In fact, human beings belong to a genus, *Homo,* which has only one living species, a situation that is perhaps not ideal in a hierarchical taxonomy. It is arguable that it is only politics that keeps *Homo* from including *Pan* and *Gorilla,* the generic names for chimpanzees and gorillas.[12] Reference will be made to several types of extinct hominids, including members of the genus *Australopithecus,* to which most of the earliest identifiable hominids belong; *Homo habilis,* the somewhat controversial candidate for earliest representative of the genus *Homo;*

Homo erectus, the species that is probably ancestral to modern humans; and to a category of humans generally called Neandertals, who had large brains but retained some primitive features of the skull, including massive browridges and a relatively flat cranial vault. Neandertals may or may not have been members of *Homo sapiens,* but they coexisted in time with human beings who were clearly modern. Note that figure 5, which shows the relationships among these hominid species, does not represent them in terms of a tree diagram. Instead, each species is shown as a band occupying a certain time frame. This sort of diagram more accurately represents the state of knowledge about the interrelationships among these species than would a tree diagram. For most of the past fifty years, paleoanthropologists have debated the question whether there was a time when two or more species of hominids were alive contemporaneously or whether hominids are monophyletic, representing a single lineage. The majority opinion now favors sev-

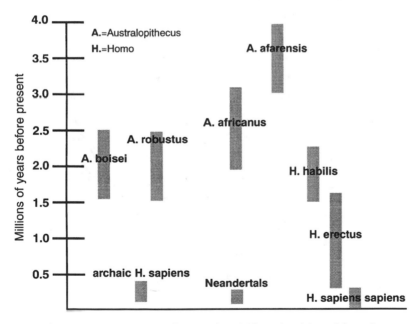

Fig. 5. Approximate time spans of various hominid species. Adapted from diagrams and data in Corballis, *Lopsided Ape,* and Tattersall, *Fossil Trail.*

eral coexisting species of australopithecines and perhaps more than one lineage within the genus *Homo*. However, the relationships among all of the possible species are far from being understood clearly.

Because of the new information provided by DNA analysis, there is currently a movement among taxonomists to include the great apes, including chimpanzees, gorillas, and sometimes orangutans, in the family Hominidae, along with human beings. These apes would thus, in future, be called hominids along with living and extinct humans. Figures 6 and 7 illustrate the traditional view of the relationships among humans and apes and this newer view based on the DNA evidence.[13] The human lineage, after its separation from the African apes, would be included in a separate subfamily the Homininae, and living and extinct humans would be called homin*ine*s to distinguish them from homin*id*s. While this may be a taxonomically satisfying approach, it introduces terminological difficulties and confusion;[14] this book will employ the traditional usage of the term *hominid* as referring only to the

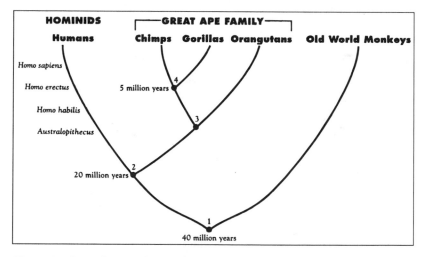

Fig. 6. Traditional view of the evolutionary relationships among apes and humans. Reprinted, by permission of the publisher, from *Next of Kin* by Roger Fouts with Stephen Tukel Mills (New York: William Morrow and Co. and Michael Joseph/Penguin Books Ltd., 1997), p. 53. © 1997 by Roger Fouts.

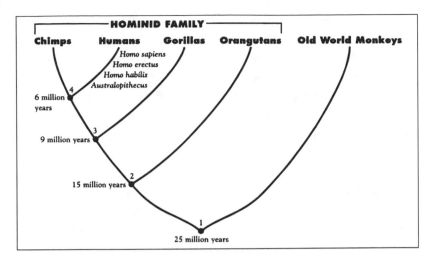

Fig. 7. Newer view of evolutionary relationships among apes and humans based on DNA analysis. Reprinted, by permission of the publisher, from *Next of Kin* by Roger Fouts with Stephen Tukel Mills (New York: William Morrow and Co. and Michael Joseph/Penguin Books Ltd., 1997), p. 56. © 1997 by Roger Fouts.

human lineage after its separation from the African apes, that is, to the genera *Australopithecus* and *Homo*. Disagreements also exist about the proper nomenclature to apply to various fossil human remains and to the evolutionary relationships among them. The reader should be aware that the evolutionary grade referred to here as *Homo erectus* includes fossils that have been given other names, such as *Homo ergaster* and *Homo heidelbergensis*. These fossils may represent intermediate forms between *Homo erectus* and earlier or later human species, or they may represent separate lineages.[15] Here the approach will be simply to refer to the smallest possible number of putative members of genus *Homo: Homo habilis, Homo erectus,* and *Homo sapiens.*

The anthropologist and primatologist John Napier presents a list of evolutionary trends among the primates that bear directly on the contention that visual-gestural communication may have been a precursor of language.[16] This list is based on one previously developed by the great British anatomist and paleoanthropologist Wilfrid Le Gros Clark, and a portion of its elements are included here:

1. Preservation of a generalized structure of the limbs with a primitive pentadactyly and the retention of certain elements of the skeleton (such as the clavicle) which tend to be reduced or to disappear in some groups of mammals.
2. An enhancement of the free mobility of the digits especially the thumb and big toe (which are used for grasping purposes).
3. The replacement of sharp, compressed claws by flattened nails associated with the development of highly sensitive tactile pads on the digits.
4. The elaboration and perfection of the visual apparatus with development of varying degrees of binocular vision.
5. Progressive elaboration of the brain affecting predominantly the cerebral cortex and its dependencies.
6. Progressive development of truncal uprightness leading to a facultative bipedalism.

To put this information into context, one must understand that the primary adaptation of the primates that explains these trends is arboreal—that is, to life in trees involving clinging and leaping, and the capture and manipulation of small food items such as insects and fruit. The primary sensory adaptation of the primates is, thus, visual. One should also note that these are all characteristics of the hominids, especially the last two. In fact, it is impossible to overemphasize the importance of the last two trends in human evolution. Upright bipedalism, the defining characteristic of the hominids, is unique among the mammals and precedes, in the fossil record, the enlargement of the brain beyond what is seen in chimpanzees. It is not hard to see how this posture, combined with a generalized hand capable of full opposition of the fingers to the thumb (see fig. 8), would be critical to the development of a characteristically visual-gestural mode of communication. Bipedalism frees the hands from locomotor functions for use in gesture and toolmaking, and upright posture causes the body to be in full view of conspecifics (members of the same species) and thus usable as a point of reference and origin for a variety of gestures.

Chimpanzees, in many ways, appear to be intermediate between quadrupedal primates and bipedal human beings, and they exhibit enlarged brains and complex social behavior. Their characteristic mode of locomotion, often described as "knuckle walking with brachiation," involves partially or fully upright pos-

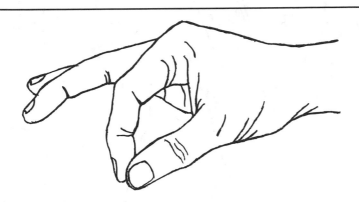

The essential component of both power and precision grips is the thumb. The mass of muscle at the base of the thumb, known as the mount of Venus or more prosaically the ball of the thumb, is composed of a series of small muscles that acting together produce a rotary movement by which the thumb swings inward towards the palm. This movement is known as *opposability*. For the movement to be of functional significance the thumb must oppose something. In man, the most precise function that the hand is capable of is to place the tip of the thumb in *opposition* to the tip of the index finger so that the pulps of the two digits make maximum contact. In this position, small objects can be manipulated with an unlimited potential for fine pressure adjustments or minute directional corrections. Opposition, to this degree of precision, is a hallmark of mankind. No nonhuman primate can replicate it. Although most people are unaware of the evolutionary significance of this finger-thumb opposition they cannot be unaware of its implications in international sign language; it is the universal gesture of human success. (Napier, *Roots of Mankind,* 181)

Fig. 8. The precision grip in human beings. Redrawn by Robert C. Johnson from Napier, *Roots of Mankind,* 181.

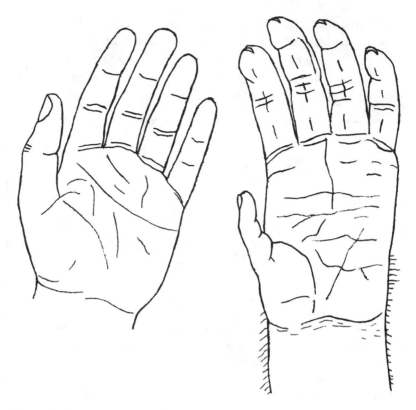

Fig. 9. The hands of chimpanzees and humans. Redrawn by Robert C. Johnson from Napier, *Roots of Mankind,* 148.

ture, with accompanying specializations of the hand and upper body. Most of the other anthropoid primates (i.e., monkeys) are plantigrade quadrupeds, meaning that they walk with the palms of their hands and the soles of their feet flat on the ground. Compared to these monkeys, chimpanzees and gorillas have long arms, short legs, and long, curved fingers. When they walk they place the knuckles of their hands on the ground, while their feet are plantigrade, hence the term *knuckle walking* to describe their mode of locomotion. Because their arms and trunks are relatively long and their legs short, their characteristic posture is partly upright. Chimpanzees also do a great deal of tree climbing and are capable of brachiation, that is, arm swinging, hand over hand, with the hands acting like hooks. Gorillas, although presumably adapted to this mode of locomotion at some time in their history, have grown too heavy to spend much time in the trees. This adaptation of the hand in chimpanzees means that they lack some of the fine manipulation skill that humans have, including the ability to oppose the thumb to the other fingers fully (see fig. 9). This limits the ability of chimpanzees to mimic some characteristic human abilities, including manual signing. Finally, chimpanzees differ from human beings with respect to the configuration of their vocal tracts and the musculature of their faces. In general, chimpanzees do not seem to have the same level of voluntary control over the muscles of the vocal tract that is possessed by human beings, they are not able to produce the same range of vocal sounds, and their facial musculature does not provide for as much expressive gesture.

The idea that the behavior of modern chimpanzees might be an acceptable model for the behavior of early hominids requires some justification. The fossil record tells us that the earliest undoubted hominids, members of the genus, *Australopithecus,* had brains that were roughly the size of those of modern chimpanzees; and, as we have already seen, from a genetic point of view chimpanzees are the closest living relatives of modern *Homo sapiens.* However, chimpanzees are not simply primitive human beings. They have had their own separate evolutionary history during the roughly five to six million years that have passed since their ancestral lineage separated from our own. Nevertheless, several pieces of evidence lead to the conclusion that, from an evolutionary perspective, chimpanzees have been relatively conservative, and have changed much less than human beings since the lineages split. Two fundamental bases support this supposition, both of which are open to criticism because of the lack of direct fossil evidence, particularly postcranial evidence from the time of the hypothesized division of the lineages. First is the genetic evidence that human beings and chimpanzees are more closely related to each other than either is to gorillas. Because both chimpanzees and gorillas are knuckle walkers, it is inferred that the common ancestor of chimpanzees and humans must also have been one. Otherwise, that very peculiar locomotor adaptation would have had to evolve independently in the chimp and gorilla lineages, a very improbable possibility. Second, given disputed evidence that the common ancestor inhabited rain forest or mixed woodlands and chimpanzees continue to do so, it is inferred that chimpanzees would have been under less evolutionary pressure than hominids, who presumably moved into more open and challenging environments.[17]

Given these arguments, it has seemed reasonable to use evidence about the "linguistic" capacities of chimpanzees to make inferences about the linguistic behavior of the earliest hominids. The evidence that has been collected includes experimental evidence involving the teaching of various kinds of linguistic systems to chimpanzees, including speech, signed language, and invented symbol systems. What this evidence actually proves, if anything, has been the subject of heated debate, and claims have been made that were probably unwarranted. However, we should not do what Steven Pinker does in *The Language Instinct* and simply disparage studies of chimpanzees that attempt to discover the limits of their abilities to exhibit "humanlike," especially linguistic, behavior.[18] Surely no other way exists to gain additional insight into what the linguistic capabilities of the earliest hominids might have been.

So what is actually known about the cognitive and communicative capabilities of chimpanzees? In what ways are chimpanzees similar to human beings, and in what ways are they different? In their book, *Gesture and the Nature of Language,* Armstrong, Stokoe, and Wilcox summarize the findings from experimental studies as follows:

> First, trainers have had more success teaching chimpanzees manual signs than spoken words. However, this requires considerable qualification—the hands of chimpanzees are very different from

those of humans. Chimpanzees have only semi-opposable thumbs and their fingers are long and curved. Consequently, they can only form approximations to many ASL handshapes. It is also apparent that it is easy for trainers to mold the hands of chimpanzees into desired shapes, while the vocal apparatus is not easily molded in this way. The techniques of modern speech pathology have apparently never been tried with chimpanzees, so in fact little is actually known about the *capacity* of chimpanzees to acquire speech under training. Second, it is clear that chimpanzees have well-developed capabilities to learn and use signs (symbols, icons, indices) to communicate with humans and with other chimpanzees. Third, although they can form these signs into short strings, they appear not to be capable of complex syntactic abilities, although there are recent claims of "proto-grammar" in pygmy chimps [often called bonobos].[19]

Considerable recent evidence concerning the natural communicative behavior of chimpanzees in the wild has also emerged. What is perhaps most notable about this is the obvious volubility of feral chimpanzees—almost all field investigators have commented on how loud they are and on how constant is the noise that they make. But this may have led some investigators to focus too much on the vocal communication of chimps and not enough on their natural gestural communication, because they also exhibit many visual gestures of dominance, submission, and so forth that are easily understood by human beings. This gestural repertoire was once believed not to include pointing, but there is now good evidence among chimpanzees for spontaneous use of this very characteristic human behavior.[20] Chimpanzees thus seem to provide a model of behavior that is just one step down from true linguistic behavior—the missing ingredient being, perhaps, syntax.

The fossil record of the earliest hominids suggests several additional things about the origin of language. Most important was an observation made above—bipedalism is the defining characteristic of the hominids, and appears before the expansion of the brain. With bipedalism came the very early evolution of the human hand into essentially its modern configuration. In fact, the postcranial skeleton of *Homo erectus,* a species that appeared more than one million years ago, is essentially indistinguishable from that of modern human beings. So, with respect to fully upright posture and the anatomy of the hands, *Homo erectus* was fully modern. What is different about this species, and what distinguishes it from *Homo sapiens,* is the smallness of its cranium (see fig. 10), the primitive appearance of its facial anatomy, and the inference that its vocal tract has not become capable of the full range of sounds made by modern humans. With respect to the so-called "classic" Neandertals who coexisted with modern *Homo sapiens* up until about thirty thousand years ago, the controversial claim has been made that, although they had brains as large as those of modern humans, they retained some of the primitive characteristics of the vocal tract, and may thus have had less capacity for articulate speech than modern *Homo sapiens.* Controversy also continues over whether Neandertals should be considered a separate species of hominids or merely a subspecies of *Homo sapiens.*

Taking all of this evidence together, several inferences can be drawn about the probable communicative capacities of the various grades of hominids. First, the communicative behavior of the earliest representatives of *Australopithecus* was probably quite similar to that of modern chimpanzees, involving both the vocal and visual-gestural channels. Second, as their brains increased in size, hominid communicative behavior came increasingly under voluntary control and became more complex, with the visual-gestural channel carrying most of the increase in complexity. Third, as the level of archaic *Homo sapiens* was reached, perhaps four hundred thousand years ago, the vocal channel became the predominant channel for linguistic communication, but the use of the visual-gestural channel for this purpose was never abandoned. In fact, it continues to be the predominant channel for deaf people and others for whom vocal communication is either impossible or impractical. It is also interesting to note that well-developed signed systems have been found in use, either as adjuncts to or substitutes for speech, among preliterate, especially hunter-gatherer, societies in large parts of the world where such societies survived into modern times, especially in Australia, Africa, and the Americas. Moreover, complex gestural communication continues to accompany the speech of hearing people everywhere. Speech and sign became inextricably bound together during the evolutionary history of the human species, and this has profound implications for how we should think about language in general.

Terrence Deacon acknowledges the complex interrelationship between gesture and speech in his 1997 book, *The Symbolic Species;*

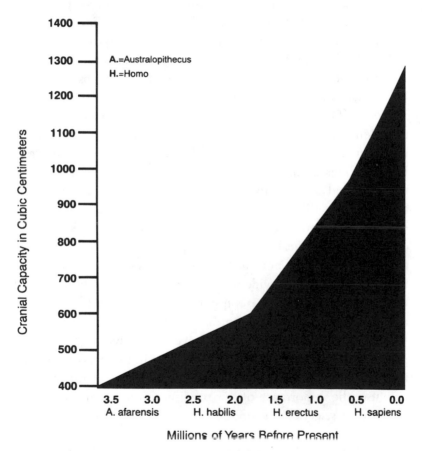

Fig. 10. Increase in cranial capacity for putative ancestors of modern humans. Adapted from a diagram in Bickerton, *Language and Species,* 135.

however, he argues against the idea of a stage in human evolutionary history in which communication was primarily in the visual-gestural channel. Because Deacon's discussion of the evolution of language is otherwise so cogent, it is worth discussing in some detail his objections to a significant role for something like signed language in this history. According to Deacon, the case against signed language rests on two basic premises: first, certain significant genetically based human adaptations can be explained only as adaptations to the use of speech; second, no such adaptations can be explained as adaptations to the use of sign. Deacon claims that substantial coevolution, in the hominid line, of spoken language and certain neurological and perceptual traits has occurred. Coevolution or "Baldwinian evolution" as Deacon terms it, after a turn-of-the-century evolutionary psychologist, James Mark Baldwin, can be understood as genetic change involving a sort of positive feedback relationship between a highly adaptive behavioral complex and the neurological or anatomical characteristics that support it. It has been shown, for example, that human beings are predisposed to distinguish among certain closely related sounds that are found in speech simply by the amount of time between the start of consonant sound production and the onset of vocal sound. As Deacon notes, this could be taken as evidence of a "genetically assimilated, perceptual motor adaptation for language, were it not for the fact that this same temporal delay has been found to provide a categorical perceptual boundary in other species as well." Deacon goes on to argue that "[t]his does not imply that genetic assimilation was totally uninvolved. Rather, it indicates that languages have taken advantage of predispositions for sound analysis already present in the nervous system, recruiting them for this special purpose. Because of this habitual new use, the importance of this predisposition has increased, and Baldwinian selection has undoubtedly enhanced both its analysis and production."[21]

As we will see in a later chapter, this argument has important implications for claims that have been made about the genetic basis for aspects of the human capacity for language. However, the second half of Deacon's argument against an evolutionary role for signed language requires our attention here:

> If something analogous to American Sign Language long predated spoken languages and served as the bridge linking the communication processes of our relatively inarticulate ancestors, then we should expect that a considerable period of Baldwinian evolution would have specialized both the production and the perception of manual gestures. Clearly there are some nearly universal gestures associated with pointing, begging, threatening, and so on, but these more closely resemble the nonlinguistic gestural communication of other primates both in their indexical functions and in the sorts of social relationships they encode, rather than anything linguistic or symbolic. The absence of other similarly categorical and modularized gestural predispositions suggests, in comparison to speech specializations, that the vast majority of Baldwinian evolution for language has taken place with respect to speech. Pointing may be the exception that proves the rule. This universal gesture exhibits many features which suggest that its production and interpretation are subject to innate predispositions. The fact that it appears prior to language as a powerful form of social communication in children (but not in other primates), and subsequently plays a very powerful role in children's language development, is particularly relevant evidence that it traced a complementary evolutionary path with the evolution of speech. The way it is recruited into manually signed languages and recoded symbolically for use as a pronomial marker with respect to signing position in space (among other uses distinct from its nonlinguistic indexical role) demonstrates how such a predisposition might have enhanced the ease with which it entered symbolic communication in the past in languages that were somewhat less verbally facile.[22]

Anyone arguing that signed language played an important role in the evolution of human language generally might be tempted at this point to say, "Well, yes, . . . but. . . ." Indeed, there is much in the quoted paragraph that needs clarification. First, we have already considered several reasons for believing that the visual-gestural channel might once have been primary in human communication, and Deacon deals with none of these. Second, he presents no evidence to support his contention that there are no significant human genetic adaptations to the use of gesture. Given the powerful visual apparatus that we inherited, it is not clear what further refinements in visual perception might have been needed, but there is reason to believe that our primate ancestors may have had genetic predispositions to the perception of gesture in the form of neural circuits specially tuned to respond to visual displays characterized as "reach for, retrieve, manipulate, pick, tear, present, and hold."[23] Such neural circuitry has been found in monkeys. Moreover, there is reason to believe that the degree of manual dexterity found in humans may have coevolved with gestural communication. How else can we explain the human ability to learn a piano sonata, especially first to perceive it visually and then to translate it from the linear strings of symbolic markings on pages of music to incredibly rapid and complex muscular actions of fingers, hands, and arms? Are several million years making crude stone tools sufficient to explain this ability? More insight might be gained by watching deaf people signing to one another. Just as no other animal possesses the human facility for rapidly producing and apprehending speech sounds, no other animal possesses this degree of manual dexterity. In this regard, it is interesting to consider the results of research conducted by I. King Jordan, a professor of psychology and later president of Gallaudet University. Jordan tested a number of factors as possible predictors of success for adults learning sign language as a second language. The most reliable predictor he was able to identify was sensitivity to rhythm.[24]

Finally, with respect to the assertion that pointing is simply "recruited" into signed languages and "recoded" symbolically, it is necessary to note that this issue is exceedingly complex. After years of painstaking research, Scott Liddell, an ASL linguist working at Gallaudet University, has concluded that, despite the promulgation of this claim in the psycholinguistic literature, evidence suggests that when pointing gestures are used in some contexts in ASL they remain just that—pointing gestures. Liddell proposes that in these contexts, pointing is used by signers much the way it is used by hearing speakers.[25] But more about this last "point" later. Moreover, as we saw earlier, chimpanzees sometimes *do* use pointing gestures, contrary to the often repeated assertion that they do not.

Another human trait that seems integral to spoken language illustrates nicely the problem raised by Stephen J. Gould in assuming that one necessarily understands the selective pressures that may have been at work in human evolution. This particular trait is one that is frequently given as an example of coevolution between spoken language and the anatomical systems that support it. The human upper respiratory system is quite different from that of other primates. In most mammals, the passage from the mouth to the larynx is relatively straight and short, the larynx being high up in the neck. The high position of the larynx allows for separate passages for food and air, and as a consequence, death by choking is rare. However, because this pattern results in a small supralaryngeal pharynx, only a small range of sounds can be produced. In adult humans, on the other hand, the larynx occupies a much lower level in the neck due to a flexing of the base of the cranium. This has two principal effects: it creates a much larger pharynx, increasing the range of vowel sounds that can be produced; but, at the same time, it creates a common pathway for food and air, greatly increasing the risk of death by choking. The illustrations in figure 11 show the difference in supralaryngeal airway between chimpanzees and humans. This would seem to be a classic case of Baldwinian evolution—the descent of the larynx must be highly selected for, in support of more articulate, more readily understandable speech, to overcome the deleterious effects that it also introduces. However, the reasons for this evolutionary change are problematic. It also turns out that the basicranial flexion associated with the descent of the larynx is a natural response to the development of upright posture. In a pronograde quadruped (a quadruped that walks with its body parallel to the ground) the head is slung forward in front of the body, and the spinal column

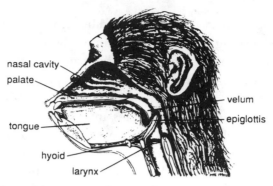

A typical nonhuman supralaryngeal airway: a chimpanzee. The tongue is positioned entirely within the oral cavity; the larynx is positioned high, close to the opening to the nose. The epiglottis and velum overlap to form a watertight seal when the larynx is raised, locking into the nose during feeding. The hyoid bone is connected to the larynx, jawbone, and skull by means of muscles and ligaments; it is part of the anatomical system that can raise the larynx.

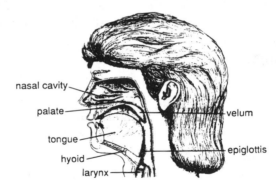

The supralaryngeal airway of an adult human being. The low position of the larynx makes it impossible for it to lock into the nose. The tongue has a very different shape from those of all other terrestrial mammals; its posterior contour is almost round in this lateral view and forms both the floor of the oral cavity and the front part of the pharynx.

Fig. 11. Vocal tracts of chimpanzees and humans. Reprinted, by permission of the publisher, from *Uniquely Human* by Philip Lieberman (Cambridge, Mass: Harvard University Press, 1991). Copyright © 1991 by the President and Fellows of Harvard College. Illustration by Matthew Carrano.

exits the skull through an opening, known as the foramen magnum, relatvely far back on the skull. In an upright biped, the skull must balance on the top of the spinal column, so the foramen magnum is at the base of a skull that has been bent forward and upward. The relatively low position of the larynx may simply be a biomechanical by-product of the ongoing perfection of upright bipedalism.[26] If that is true, then the enlarged human pharynx would, quite literally, be simply a spandrel.

If we are to speculate that the visual-gestural channel was once predominant in human linguistic communication (and we are certainly going to do that here), it becomes necessary to speculate about the reasons that speech now occupies this position. The reasons that have been put forward, based in common sense, are exceptionally mundane:

1. Speech projects past opaque objects.
2. Speech does not require directed attention on the part of the hearer.
3. Speech leaves the hands free for work or carrying.
4. Speech may be more energy efficient than signing.
5. Speech can be used in the dark.

It seems almost farcical to propose this last reason, but many people in modern society forget that up until about a century ago, the bulk of humanity had spent roughly 50 percent of its time in the dark for several million years.

Is it advisable to speculate in more detail about how early hominids lived, thought, and communicated? The answer to this question is a qualified yes, but, again, we should avoid the teleological trap of imagining that their behavioral repertoires were stages along the way to full-blown human language and culture. These were successful animals that lived for millennia using adaptations that must have been substantially different from those of modern human beings. Several anthropological classics contain attempts to explain "primitive" thought to Western society—prominent among these are works of Claude Lévi-Strauss and Franz Boas.[27] For the most part, these attempts have been motivated by the need to counteract racist interpretations of "primitive" behavior by showing that the intellectual capacities and thought processes of Western and non-Western members of *Homo sapiens* are the same in all important respects. While this assumption may or may not be valid, it is much more challenging to attempt to come to grips with the behavior of our extinct ancestors who were animals that, while like us in many important respects, nevertheless differed from us in fundamental ways.

Merlin Donald has made a recent comprehensive attempt to reconstruct the behavior of various extinct hominid species in his book *Origins of the Modern Mind*. This attempt succeeds in many respects, to the extent that Donald seriously applies many of the principles that were enumerated above. He begins with what we have already seen to be a reasonable assumption: that because the overall body size and cranial capacity of modern chimpanzees are similar to those of the earliest known hominids, one can reasonably assume that the cognitive capacities of these early hominids might have been similar to those of chimps also. He goes on to speculate that the cultural life of *Australopithecus* was what he calls "episodic," and then builds on what is known about the lifestyles of other hominid species from the fossil evidence for their anatomy and the archaeological evidence for their material culture. Donald describes the "episodic" culture of the australopithecines in terms of what is known about the behavior of apes:

> Their lives are lived entirely in the present, as a series of concrete episodes, and the highest element in their system of representation seems to be at the level of event representation. Where humans have abstract symbolic memory representations, apes are bound to the concrete situation or episode; and their social behavior reflects this situational limitation. Their culture might be therefore classified as an episodic culture.[28]

Here Donald appears to have underestimated the capacity of African apes for planning and for complex social living—in fact, there is abundant evidence that chimpanzees live in fluid and long-lasting social groups that must involve sophisticated planning and organizational skills[29]—but we will give him credit for a good faith effort to use phylogenetically relevant information. According to Donald, the culture of *Homo erectus* can be described as "mimetic." Donald speculates that mimesis preceded true language, and he defines it in the following terms to distinguish it from the imitation and mimicry of which apes are clearly capable: "[M]imesis is fundamentally different from imitation and mimicry in that it involves the *invention* of intentional representations." Donald also speculates that "generativity," "the ability to 'parse' one's own motor actions into components and then recombine these components in various ways," may also be aspects of mimetic culture.[30] We will explore this possibility in great detail in chapter 4. Although these later developments in human behavior are not explored in depth in this book, it should be noted that Donald goes on to describe the evolution of the culture of *Homo sapiens* in terms of "mythic" culture evolving into the culture of literacy.

To put all of this speculation in perspective and to further guard against inevitable reversions to teleology, the reader is invited to participate in a simple thought experiment. To borrow and alter a phrase from Oliver Sacks, what if "anthropologists from Mars" had come to Earth at various times in the past—say 3,000,000, 1,000,000, 100,000, and 20,000 years ago.[31] What would these Martian visitors have concluded about the potential of the hominids, *our* potential? What would they have predicted about our future? In their first visit they would have found upright apes with extremely simple tools, confined to the continent of Africa, probably without clothing and fire. These creatures, they would note on their second visit (with a little archaeological investigation), hung on in much this state for at least 1,000,000 years, to be replaced by taller, (probably) hairless (except for their heads and certain other strategic locations), upright creatures whose tools did not appear much more complex but who now, perhaps, possessed clothing, controlled fire, and had begun to spread throughout much of the African, European, and Asian continents. Would these Martian visitors have predicted that these creatures, with their unimpressive tool kits, were closer in time to descendants who would walk on the moon than they were to the apelike ancestors that they had first visited?

On their next visit, our anthropologists would have found a curious looking hominid, somewhat shorter than its predecessor and with extraordinary musculature. This hominid had a very large brain but a fairly primitive looking skull with massive browridges and a low, flat cranial vault. They would also have found other hominids, primarily in Africa, who looked much like modern human beings. All would have been skilled at communicating with one another, either in sign language or speech, or most likely some combination of the two. Although there would be some improvement in the basic tool kits of both kinds of hominids, there would still not be much to separate them technologically from the hominids of 900,000 years earlier.

On their final visit, the Martian anthropologists would have found hominids indistinguishable from us, inhabiting most of the world. But the Martians, who had been capable of space flight for 3,000,000 years, would have been extremely underwhelmed with the hominids' still very simple technology. These hominids would still not be in full control of the production of food and would still be living in small, widely dispersed bands and without permanent habitation. And, given that they were the products of a very refined Martian culture (for details see Robert Heinlein's *Stranger in a Strange Land*), our anthropologists would have been either amused by or revolted at the hominids' constant chattering and gesticulation. There would still be little sign of an incipient capacity for development of the technology needed for space travel. Although these hominids possessed a relatively unimpressive material technology, our perceptive Martian anthropologists would be fairly impressed with their ability to organize themselves for productive group activities through the use of their face-to-face communication system.

After returning to the present, the reader is offered what the French might call a *mode d'emploi*—directions for using this book. What will be considered here is not a scenario for or a story about the emergence of language in the hominid line. Rather, this book will examine several topics fundamental to an understanding of language with the goal of illuminating them in the light of current information about language in the visual modality and the probable evolutionary history of the hominids, especially as this history relates to the biological capacity for language. It is not strictly necessary, therefore, to read the subsequent chapters sequentially, although several of the arguments will be clearer if that course is taken.

Notes

1. Hewes (1976, 483).
2. Gallaudet (1983, 211).
3. King and Shanker (1997) argue that the dichotomy between "continuity" and "discontinuity" is too simplistic to fully characterize the diversity of opinion that now exists in the field of language origins. However, it does seem to point to an important underlying ideological difference.
4. Stokoe (1965).
5. Hewes (1976).
6. Wescott, Hewes, and Stokoe (1974); Hockett (1978).
7. Wilcox (1996).
8. Stokoe (1980).
9. Bickerton (1990); Deacon (1997).
10. Bickerton (1990).
11. For clear presentations of recent evidence see Diamond (1992, 18–31) and Fouts and Mills (1997, 51–59).
12. See Diamond (1992, 25).
13. Fouts and Mills (1997, 51–59).
14. See Tattersall (1995, 126).
15. For an excellent and very readable discussion of the many controversies surrounding the classification of fossil hominids, see Tattersall (1995).
16. Napier and Napier (1967, 6).
17. For evidence that the common ancestors of chimps and humans looked much like a chimp, see Begun (1994).

18. Pinker (1994, 341).

19. Armstrong, Stokoe, and Wilcox (1995); see also recent books by Sue Savage-Rumbaugh (1994), Roger Fouts and Stephen Mills (1997), and Barbara King (1994).

20. Leavens et al. (1996).

21. Deacon (1997, 361–62).

22. Ibid. (362).

23. Perrett et al. (1987; 1989).

24. Mills and Jordan (1980).

25. Liddell (1996).

26. Buettner-Janusch (1966, 337). Gibson (1997) argues that the anatomical differences in the upper respiratory tract between humans and other primates have been exaggerated.

27. Lévi-Strauss (1962); Boas ([1911] 1963).

28. Donald (1991, 149).

29. See Armstrong, Stokoe, and Wilcox (1995, 215–23) for a summary of this evidence.

30. Donald (1991, 169, 171).

31. Sacks (1995). Extraterrestrials, especially Martians, have a long history of participation in thought experiments about the nature of language (see Pinker, 1994, 231–42; Sarles, 1974).

2 | The Rage to Order

AT THE BEGINNING of a book about the origin, evolution, and nature of language, it is appropriate to ask these questions: What is the most basic purpose of language, and what is its most essential property? The answers to these questions may seem obvious, but in a book that is devoted to examining the potential of language in various modalities, these questions are extremely important. The first question has several possible answers, but the one to be explored in this book is that language exists to serve the communication needs of human beings—to enable social action. That language is a powerful cognitive agent, an enabler of thought, is also clear, but the assumption here is that language is first and foremost the means by which human beings communicate with their fellows.

Some would argue that for human beings to communicate meaningfully about the world, they must first partition it into manageable categories. Without categorization and conceptualization, the world would appear to us, to borrow a phrase from William James, as "one great blooming, buzzing confusion."[1] This suggests an answer to the second question posed at the beginning of the previous paragraph. An ordering and classifying principle would thus be the basis for all human mental activity. According to Claude Lévi-Strauss in *The Savage Mind:*

> Now, this need to order is the basis for all thought that we call primitive, but only to the extent that it is the basis for all thought: because it is under the guise of their common properties that we have ready access to forms of thought that seem foreign to us.[2]

The ordering process that Lévi-Strauss is concerned with is ordering in terms of assignment to categories and the placing of these categories in hierarchical or temporal sequences. The idea that categorizing and ordering are the most important prerequisites for human thought, and ultimately language, is frequently expressed. The most elementary characteristic of "primitive" thought is often said to be binary or categorical opposition, by writers as diverse as Carl Jung and Lévi-Strauss.[3] Binary contrast of this sort is, of course, at the heart of traditional structural linguistics as formulated by the likes of Ferdinand de Saussure and Roman Jakobson. Beginning with Franz Boas,[4] the founder of the modern American discipline, anthropologists have also posited the ability to classify as the precursor of the entire human cognitive efflorescence. In general, once some primitive form of language begins to develop, language itself, and the particular way of segmenting the world that each language implies, is then seen as the major force guiding human thought and behavior.

In a book that deals with the unique role manual communication may have played in the development of the human mind, it is perhaps justifiable to include an aside about the work, early in the twentieth century, of the French *sociologue* Robert Hertz. Hertz saw the basis of human binary classification systems in the regularity of thought, across cultures, about the roles of the two hands and the values assigned to them:

> What resemblance more perfect than that between our two hands! And yet what a striking inequality there is! To the right hand go honors, flattering designations, prerogatives: it acts, orders, and takes. The left hand, on the contrary, is despised and reduced to the role of humble auxiliary: by itself it can do nothing; it supports, it holds.[5]

People familiar with ASL may find this pancultural description of the roles of the two hands to be a good account of how the hands are used to produce ASL utterances.

The poet Wallace Stevens gives us a particularly powerful statement of the human ordering principle in some famous lines from the "The Idea of Order at Key West":

> The maker's rage to order words of the sea,
> Words of the fragrant portals, dimly-starred,
> And of ourselves and of our origins,
> In ghostlier demarcations, keener sounds.

Here, the ordering, categorizing, defining principle of mind is brilliantly illuminated and related specifically to language as the organizing agent. But how is this ordering and categorizing carried out, and is it done the same way in every language? These are questions that have been addressed by two branches of linguistics that have been diverging. These branches, or approaches, may be referred to, after their two best-known proponents, as "Chomskyan" and "Whorfian." More generally, the approaches to the study of language implied by this bifurcation may be characterized as formal and anthropological linguistics, respectively. Some would probably object to the characterization of anthropological linguistics as Whorfian, but what is intended here is not a rigorous historical analysis, but an attempt to illuminate two quite divergent ways of viewing language and its relation to human thought and culture.

To understand this divergence, one must first consider the common intellectual basis of all modern approaches to linguistics, which is usually said to have begun with Ferdinand de Saussure early in the twentieth century. Saussure was a Swiss professor of linguistics whose lecture notes were published by his students following his early death. Prior to Saussure, the organized study of language in its own right tended to be historical and was generally known as philology—the systematic study of the historical relationships among languages, generally through the study of sound and meaning correspondences. The first great achievement of this field in the late eighteenth and early nineteenth centuries was the discovery that almost all of the languages of Europe and India were related and belonged to a single family of languages, now known as Indo-European.[6]

Three principal ideas about language attributed to Saussure are important here because they signified the beginning of a new approach to the study of language. First is the idea that linguistic signs are arbitrary, bearing no necessary relationship to the things for which they stand. Signs in this context are understood to mean words. This idea, that words are symbols, is, of course, not new with Saussure—Shakespeare gave what is probably the most famous statement of it: "What's in a name? That which we call a rose by any other name would smell as sweet." Saussure insisted on this as one of the basic properties of language, and its incorporation into the dogma of scientific linguistics has posed a major problem for the linguistics of signed languages, as we will see in the next chapter. Second is the distinction between *langue* and *parole,* or language as a formal system (*langue*) and its imperfect realization in actual speech (*parole*). This second principle introduces Platonism into linguistics, as it comes to see as its subject the ideal form of language, rather than the statistical study of language as it is actually used in face-to-face interaction. Thus linguists become grammarians, rather than social scientists. Third is Saussure's distinction between synchronic and diachronic processes in language. The idea of synchronic study is closely allied with the idea of *la langue,* that is, the study of the ideal form of a language at a particular point in time (synchronicity) as opposed to the study of historical change in language (diachronicity). After Saussure, much of the emphasis in linguistics shifted from historical or diachronic study to synchronic study—the study of the current forms of the world's languages.[7]

Emerging at roughly the time that Saussure was giving his lectures (the turn of the twentieth century) was the field of anthropological linguistics. This endeavor, especially in North America, was seen initially as an emergency salvage operation to preserve, on paper and audio recordings when possible, the languages of aboriginal peoples believed to be on their way to extinction. This effort of anthropological linguistics had a certain poignancy and a certain urgency, perhaps best exemplified by the case of Ishi, the last speaker of the Yahi language of California. Ishi died while his language and aspects of his culture were being recorded by anthropologists and linguists, including Alfred Kroeber and Edward Sapir, at the anthropology museum of the University of California. The responsibility felt by many anthropological linguists is, perhaps, best stated in the account of Ishi's life given much later by Alfred Kroeber's wife, Theodora:

> It is nearly a half century since Ishi startled the Modern World by accidentally wandering into it from the Stone Age. There follows an account of all that is surely and truly known of him. What he believed and felt and did in the modern world and, earlier, in his own world are the bone beads of his story. The stringing of such of these beads as could be recovered onto a single strand has been my task. Surprisingly, the circle of his life's necklace appears whole despite its many incompletions.
>
> The history of Ishi and his people is, inexorably, part of our own history. We have absorbed their lands into our holdings. Just so must we be the responsible custodians of their tragedy, absorbing it into our tradition and morality.[8]

Under the circumstances, there should be little wonder that the efforts of anthropological linguists tended to focus on identifying the elements of the sound systems of unknown languages and the collection of word lists, or lexicons, and their corresponding meanings. These anthropologists came to realize that the languages they were studying varied vastly with respect to the elements in their lexicons, depending upon the natural and cultural circumstances with which the people in question lived. It would be remarkable indeed if Stone Age people were to have words for things like wheels, axles, and internal combustion engines. It would be equally remarkable for English-speaking inhabitants of San Francisco to have special words to distinguish their mothers' brothers from their fathers' brothers or for the plants of the New Guinea rain forest.

The technique for gathering a lexical corpus included the use of phonetic writing and from this experience emerged the concept of the phoneme, which was defined as a class of sounds, the members of which when inserted into a stream of speech sounds did not cause a difference in meaning. Alternatively, there was a phonemic difference between two sounds in a language if substitution of one for the other, in any context in the language, was capable of causing a difference in meaning, for example, /r/ and /l/ in English. The basis of the identification of a phoneme was thus binary contrast, and ordering and categorizing principles at work in human language were seen to extend below the level of the word, to a sublexical structure. Phonemes themselves were considered to be meaningless, and became meaningful only in combination. The identification of phonological rules, that is, the apparent rules in a language for assembling phonemes into meaningful units, became the basis for a science of linguistics, now generally known as structural linguistics, of which anthropological linguistics had become a subfield.

The speech sounds making up these phoneme classes could themselves be seen to have an underlying structure based on contrast or binary opposition. For example, the sound written as /p/ is distinguished, in those languages that make this distinction, from the sound written as /b/, by the fact that the latter is voiced and the former is not. According to classical structural linguistic theory, a small number of "settings" of the vocal tract accomplish the task of distinguishing all of the possible speech sounds—the so-called "distinctive features" of the phonetic system. The great Russian-born structural linguist Roman Jakobson posited that these distinctive features, described also in acoustic terms, could be described in terms of a binary matrix—each speech sound could be characterized by the presence or absence of features, such as vocalic, consonantal, voiced, nasal, discontinuous, strident, grave, and sharp. For example, the Russian phoneme /p/ could be described by the following binary vector, where (+) indicates the presence of a feature, and (−) indicates its polar opposite (e.g., (+) = voiced, (−) = voiceless):

Vocalic	−
Consonantal	+
Compact	−
Voiced	−
Nasal	−
Discontinuous	+
Grave	+
Sharp	−

In Jakobson's characterization, the act of speaking could be characterized as the production of sequences of simultaneous bundles of these distinctive features. Other classifications of distinctive features have been proposed as well, but they generally share this underlying binary logic.[9]

Anthropological linguists also recorded aspects of the grammars of the languages they were investigating, and here too were striking differences in the ways that different languages and different families of languages chose to express grammatical relationships. Some of these differences were, of course, already known to scholars of language. Even among Indo-European languages there are substantial differences in the extent to which grammatical relationships are expressed through inflection or through word order, but some languages, particularly those of Native Americans, tended to carry to an extreme the expression of relationships through internal inflection or affixation. Sapir referred to this as the language's relative degree of synthesis, and introduced three terms to describe this property: analytic, synthetic, and polysynthetic. According to Sapir:

> The terms explain themselves. An analytic language is one that either does not combine concepts into single words at all (Chinese) or does so economically (English, French). In an analytic language the sentence is always of prime importance, the word is of minor

interest. In a synthetic language (Latin, Arabic, Finnish) the concepts cluster more thickly, the words are more richly chambered, but there is a tendency, on the whole, to keep the range of concrete significance in the single word down to a moderate compass. A polysynthetic language, as its name implies, is more than ordinarily synthetic. The elaboration of the word is extreme. Concepts which we should never dream of treating in a subordinate fashion are symbolized by derivational affixes or "symbolic" changes in the radical element, while the more abstract notions, including the syntactic relations, may be conveyed by the word.[10]

Sapir also wrote that "[l]anguage is not merely a more or less systematic inventory of the various items of experience which seem relevant to the individual, as is so often naively assumed, but is also a self-contained, creative symbolic organization, which not only refers to experience largely acquired without its help but actually defines experience for us by reason of its formal completeness and because of our unconscious projection of its implicit expectations into the field of experience."[11]

So here we have the idea that both the elements in the lexicon, as well as the grammatical categories that are used to order them, might differ from language to language and that these differences might have important ramifications for the way their speakers think about the world. Although these relativistic ideas are frequently attributed to and associated with Sapir, they are most often associated with Benjamin Lee Whorf, hence the term "Whorfian," introduced above. Whorf was a Connecticut insurance executive (as, coincidentally, was Wallace Stevens) who also did much research in linguistics, including original work on Hopi and Nahuatl (the language of the Aztecs of the valley of Mexico). Whorf gives us what is perhaps the most strongly relativistic view of language's "rage to order":

> We dissect nature along lines laid down by our native languages. The categories and types that we isolate from the world of phenomena we do not find there because they stare every observer in the face; on the contrary, the world is presented in a kaleidoscope flux of impressions which has to be organized by our

minds—and this means largely by the linguistic systems in our minds. We cut nature up, organize it into concepts, and ascribe significances as we do, largely because we are parties to an agreement to organize it in this way—an agreement that holds throughout our speech community and is codified in the patterns of our language.[12]

In another passage, Whorf describes the manner in which the Hopi talk about space, including their living space in pueblos. This description will sound exceedingly familiar to anyone who is knowledgeable about American Sign Language:

> They are not set up as entities that can function in a sentence like terms for people, animals, or masses of matter having characteristic form, or again, human groups and human relations, but are treated as PURELY RELATIONAL CONCEPTS, of an adverbial type. Thus hollow spaces like room, chamber, hall, are not really NAMED as objects are, but are rather LOCATED; i.e., positions of other things are specified so as to show their location in such hollow spaces.[13]

Thus, according to Whorf, Hopi has a method different from English for classifying spaces. Another Native American language, Navaho, has a system for classifying according to object type. According to Clyde Kluckhohn, Navaho verbs have different stems, depending upon the type of object with respect to which the verb is expressing action or state. Kluckhohn gives some of the categories expressed by these stems, as follows; again, those familiar with ASL should find some of these familiar: "the long-object class (a pencil, a stick, a pipe); the slender-flexible-object class (snakes, thongs, certain pluralities including certain types of food and property); the container-*and*-contents class; the granular-mass class (sugar, salt, etc.); the things–bundled-up class (hay, bundles of clothing, etc.—if they are loose and not compact); the fabric class (paper, spread out leather, blankets, etc.); . . . and others."[14] Of course, Navaho accomplishes these classifications by means of sounds that are arbitrarily related to the categories of objects they represent, and ASL represents these classes of objects by direct, iconic resemblance (see fig. 12). Nevertheless, similar processes would seem to be at work.

Modern Indo-European languages employ some obligatory grammatical categories of this sort, as well, especially gender, but these sorts of classificatory processes do not seem to have the same importance that they do in languages like Navaho and ASL. One is, of course, tempted to see in this way of sorting the world into similar object-class or action-class categories a relationship that might reveal something about the way in which languages (and language) evolve. If we speculate that language may have emerged first as visible gesture, more than as vocal gesture, we might further hypothesize that it began much as the signed languages of people who are deaf seem to emerge, through iconic mimesis.[15] If this is true, then one might imagine that word formation involved, in its earliest stages, processes that were not vastly different from sentence formation through the active combination of mimetic elements into ever more complex gestural utterances. In a later chapter we will see how this process might have led to the elaboration of syntax, but here it is possible to see how word formation processes that originated in manual/gestural signing might have been carried over into the formation of spoken words. One

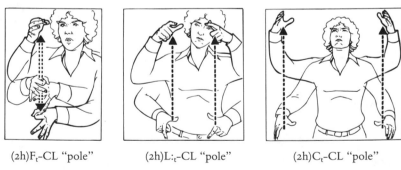

(2h)F$_t$-CL "pole"   (2h)L:$_t$-CL "pole"   (2h)C$_t$-CL "pole"

Fig. 12. ASL classifiers used to represent poles of varying widths. Reprinted, by permission of the publisher, from *American Sign Language: A Teacher's Resource Text on Grammar and Culture* by Charlotte Baker-Shenk and Dennis Cokely (Washington, D.C.: Gallaudet University Press, 1991), 310.

could imagine, for example, that classes of long, slender objects such as blades of grass or saplings might be represented by similar, iconic manual signs; and they might also be referred to by spoken words with similar classificatory roots. One can also imagine that separate, evolving groups of signers/speakers might diverge with respect to how they chose to classify their worlds through these systems of roots. Metaphoric processes would most likely also be at work.

However, the relativistic view exemplified by Whorf ran head-on into the emerging view of the generative grammarians, beginning with Chomsky. Developing shortly after the time that Whorf was refining his ideas about the profound effect of language on worldview and cognition, and then following the early deaths of both Whorf and Sapir in 1941 and 1939, respectively, was an alternate strain in the study of language. Reacting to what he saw as an almost nihilistic lack of theory and coherence in linguistics, typified by the extreme relativism of Whorf and other anthropological linguists, Noam Chomsky in the 1950s proposed a revolutionary change in the way in which language was to be studied.[16] Chomsky reacted to what appeared to be a lack of intellectual discipline in the study of language, especially the lack of a theoretical framework for understanding and predicting linguistic behavior, seemingly a fundamentally important task of a science of language.

Instead of seeing infinite diversity among languages, Chomsky was impressed with the similarities and regularities. He also argued persuasively that children could not learn their native languages simply through imitation or through an operant conditioning paradigm—that languages were too complicated and that children were exposed to only a tiny sample of the potentially infinite number of sentences that any language could encompass. As an alternative to the almost free variation based on learning simply by association that the Whorfian model seemed to suggest, Chomsky posited instead that the developing brain contained a "language organ" that was fed by a "language acquisition device." Some aspects of grammar, stated in terms of a Universal Grammar, or UG, were seen as literally wired into the brain of the developing child, so that to some extent his/her acquisition of language and the very shape of any language could be said to be genetically determined, one of the genetically determined traits of the human species.[17]

As might have been expected, this view was hotly opposed by most of the linguistic establishment, as it appeared to be a return to an abandoned mentalism, a type of psychological speculation about the inner workings of the mind not generally open to empirical testing. Anthropological linguists preoccupied with describing the seemingly endless diversity of existing languages were predictably negative toward Chomsky's emerging views. Chomsky, however, was a classic "paradigm buster",[18] and came to dominate the field of linguistics by the 1960s. These attacks on Chomsky came not only from those linguists who felt left behind by his domination of the field but also eventually from his own students. Most notably, Chomsky was attacked by students who felt that his focus was too much on a sterile, formalist, syntactic point of view, and that not enough attention was being given to the substance of language—meaning or semantics. This schism led to the creation of a field called "generative semantics,"[19] some of the ideas of which we will encounter in a later chapter dealing with William Stokoe's creation of a system called "semantic phonology."[20]

Following Chomsky's almost total victory within the field of linguistics, Sapir and Whorf fell into disfavor with professional linguists, although their work continued to be studied by anthropologists and psychologists. In fact, among the Chomskyans, Whorf became an object of ridicule. In 1973 the leading American anthropological linguist, Dell Hymes, bemoaned the fate that had befallen him:

> [L]anguages differ in their makeup as adaptive resources; the linguistic resources of speech communities differ in what can be done with them. . . . A generation ago some kinds of differences

were regarded with a spirit of relativistic tolerance, as the special virtues of the languages that had them, and so one got at least some account of their lexical and grammatical strengths. The present temper, however, treats mention of differences as grounds for suspicion of prejudice, if not racism, so that poor Whorf, who believed fervently in the universal grounding of language, and extolled the superiority of Hopi, has become, like Machiavelli, a pejorative symbol for unpleasant facts to which he called attention. [21]

What is at stake here is whether human thought is everywhere the same, or whether there are important differences that have real consequences in the lives of people from different cultures. Implicit in Chomsky's theory of the universal grounding of syntax is that anything that can be said in one language should be "effable" in any other. In fact, it was initially assumed that the theory should aid in the development of machine translation,[22] and it has been a recurring theme of Chomskyan linguists that Whorf overestimates, through his relativistic theory, the problem of translation.[23] The difference between these positions will be discussed at much greater length in chapter 6, but it should be noted here that it has profound ideological consequences.

A small digression is in order concerning Whorf's status as a whipping boy for Chomskyan linguists. Pinker's treatment of Whorf is particularly revealing because Sapir, who was at least as relativistic as Whorf, is described by Pinker as "a brilliant linguist," while Whorf's views are described as "outlandish." Why this difference in treatment? Perhaps because Sapir, at least late in his career, held a distinguished professorial chair at Yale and was president of both the American Anthropological Association and the American Linguistic Society, while Whorf was merely "an inspector for a Hartford Fire Insurance Company and an amateur scholar of Native American languages."[24] Perhaps Sapir's status as a revered founder places him a bit off limits for attack, but since his and Whorf's ideas are sensible in so many ways, the age-old tactic of the ad hominem is deployed against the academically less respectable Whorf. If the description of Whorf as an amateur is intended as a criticism, then notice should be given to the continuing resonance of his ideas within the field of anthropology.

The underlying issue often gets lost in all the sound and fury. The larger issue, in effect, concerns the intellectual status of the traditional subject matter of cultural anthropology. If everyone thinks the same way, if all languages are the same, and if every human difference is the result of an insignificant perturbation at the surface, then the anthropological enterprise has no real point. Why spend several years, sometimes under harsh physical conditions, trying to figure out what a radically foreign group of people is thinking and doing if they are really pretty much the same as us? And it is certainly true at some level that all human brains *are* wired in much the same way and that all human sensory systems process input according to largely the same principles. But the interest, at least for most anthropologists, lies and always has lain in the *details* of how such brains, acting collectively, work out solutions to the problems of survival that confront all human groups. For many of us this interest focuses particularly on languages. So, when a group of people chooses, through its language, to pay particular attention to some part or some process of the natural or social world that is not of much interest to us, it behooves *us* to pay attention to *them*.

A watchword of Chomskyan linguistics, asserted by Pinker in 1994, holds that no empirical support for the Whorfian hypothesis has ever been found.[25] Yet John Lucy, an anthropological linguist, began publishing empirical results supportive of Whorf in the 1980s, culminating with a book-length comparative study of English and Yucatec Maya in 1992.[26] Through painstaking linguistic and psychometric analysis of populations from the two language communities, Lucy was able to show that a difference in the way the two languages indicate number correlates with the ways in which their speakers habitually group objects. His general observations about the ways in which Whorfian and Chomskyan linguists have approached the business of describing language and its relationship to other aspects of behavior are instructive and worth quoting at length:

> Some advocates [of linguistic relativism] have produced sweeping and provocative formulations where relativity is assigned great significance and almost mystical qualities. In themselves, most of these claims cannot now, or perhaps ever, be proved or disproved. Indeed, the linkages of language and thought are often thought to be so pervasive and complex that no proof is possible. . . .
>
> [On the other hand,] some opponents have produced extreme, and at times absurd, formulations where relativity is seen as an inherently unprovable thesis. In one sense, those holding this position are more justified in not conducting research since they feel it is pointless. Yet such critiques cut two ways: just to the extent the hypothesis cannot be proven when formulated in this way, it also cannot be disproved. This should be a cause of deep concern to these scholars rather than a cause for satisfaction. Not to confront the implications of the issue for their own work amounts to accepting a counsel of ignorance. It would be preferable for such skeptics, even while continuing to disbelieve, to make some serious attempt to explore what truth there might be in the relativity claim—or what limits there might be to their own.[27]

Many of the issues raised by Whorf, Sapir, and Chomsky have had substantial repercussions for the way in which the signed languages of people who are deaf have been viewed. This is a highly complex issue that will be discussed in some detail in the next chapter, but certain aspects of it are important to note here. Although most deaf people have probably always recognized the legitimacy of their primary mode of communication, the history of the way it has been viewed by, at least, Western hearing people has been one of cyclical acceptance and rejection. Putting signed languages into the context of the current discussion, it could be argued that their legitimacy has been bolstered by traditional anthropological linguistics, but probably more so by the Chomskyan revolution.[28] Although anthropological linguistics fit generally within a liberal tradition of acceptance of differences, it nevertheless saw differences. Sapir, for example did not have a very high opinion of the "gesture languages of deaf-mutes," seeing them simply as codes for spoken languages.[29] In the Chomskyan system, on the other hand, signed languages could offer further proof of the universality of certain grammatical principles if these could be shown to be reproduced in a sensory medium other than the auditory. Thus, signed languages were to be welcomed into the fold, as offering the possibility of additional support for the theory. We will consider the consequences of this potential symbiosis between the dominant theory and developing descriptions of ASL throughout this book.

Last, we should not leave the topic of the human drive to conceptualize and categorize without discussing what is perhaps an even more fundamental intellectual issue that has recently been raised by the development of a new branch of formal reasoning, now known as "fuzzy logic." Despite the ideological differences that have been described in this chapter, all current approaches to linguistics are based on the idea that categorization along principles of binary opposition is fundamental to human thought and language. Fuzzy logic challenges this view by proposing that human thought is better characterized by "prototypes," categories that merge into one another, than by the sharply delimited classes of formal logic. If this view prevails, it may have relativistic implications even more profound than those introduced by Whorf.

The idea of the prototype can be illustrated by a simple example. In a study conducted by the psychologist Eleanor Rosch, American students were asked to rate, on a scale of 1 to 7, the extent to which members of various categories typified those categories.[30] The responses were then averaged. The results for the category "science" are representative:

Chemistry	1.0
Botany	1.7
Anatomy	1.7

Geology   2.6
Sociology   4.6
History   5.9

In other words, all respondents agreed that chemistry is a perfectly typical (prototypical) science, and that each of the other possible sciences is less so. One can not help wondering how linguistics would fare in such a "scientific" rating.

So, the words of a language may be seen to represent overlapping categories, but aren't the elementary sound units of language necessarily divided into discrete, clearly delineated, contrasting categories? Recent work in phonetics has undermined even this fundamental pillar of structural linguistics. Through a process called "coarticulation," it has been shown that speech sounds are influenced by the sounds that surround them. Consider the word *spoon*. In their ideal forms, the sound segments /s/, /p/, and /n/ should not have lip rounding, but because the vowel sound does, coarticulation operates to cause the lips to be rounded as pronunciation begins and remain rounded until it ends.[31] Moreover, there is also recent evidence that infants may use fuzzy logical procedures to extract the phonemes used in their language *before* they can extract meaning. The infant's task at this point in development is to recognize what is linguistically significant in the "buzzing confusion" of voices that has surrounded it from birth. Recall that the recognition of phoneme categories is supposed to depend upon recognition of differences in meaning, but according to a 1992 study:

> The results show that the initial appearance of a language specific pattern of phonetic perception does not depend on the emergence of contrastive phonology and an understanding of word meaning. Rather, infants' language-specific phonetic categories may initially emerge from an underlying cognitive capacity and proclivity to store in memory biologically important stimuli and from the ability to represent information in the form of a prototype.[32]

What is important about these results is that they show that human beings habitually group things along lines that are probabilistic and not necessarily categorical in a binary sense. As we will see later, if we accept the idea that something like the communication systems of nonhuman primates preceded language, then it may be that the first "linguistic" utterances were not like categorical words, but more like "fuzzy" sentences.

Notes

1. James ([1890]) 1983, 462).
2. Lévi-Strauss (1962, 17), translation by the author.
3. Laughlin and D'Aquili (1974, 115).
4. Boas ([1911] 1963).
5. Hertz (1909, 3).
6. See Miller (1991, 1–21).
7. See ibid.; Pinker (1994, 151–3); Greenberg (1968). What Saussure actually meant by some of these distinctions has been widely debated.
8. Kroeber (1962, frontispiece).
9. Brasington (1994).
10. Sapir (1921, 128).
11. Sapir ([1931] 1964, 578).
12. Whorf (1956, 212–13).
13. Ibid. (202). This and the previous passage from Whorf are discussed in Gill (1997, 124–43).
14. Kluckhohn and Leighton (1951, 191).
15. See Frishberg (1975); Armstrong (1983).
16. Chomsky (1957).
17. See Cook (1988); Pinker (1994).
18. In the terms of Thomas Kuhn's (1962) formulation of the course of scientific revolutions.
19. See Harris (1993).
20. Stokoe (1991).
21. Hymes (1973, 78f).
22. See, for example, Lees (1974). However, Chomsky (1965, 30) himself states explicitly, in *Aspects of the Theory of Syntax,* that his theory does not imply "that there must be some reasonable procedure for translating between languages."
23. Pinker (1994, 59–64).
24. Ibid. (59–63).
25. Ibid. (65–67).
26. Lucy (1992).

27. Ibid. (153–54).

28. See Neisser (1983) for a discussion of the relationship between the Chomsky revolution in linguistics and recognition of the legitimacy of ASL.

29. Sapir (1921, 21).

30. See McNeill and Freiberger (1993, 84–85).

31. See Armstrong, Stokoe, and Wilcox (1995, 8–11).

32. Kuhl et al. (1992, 608).

3 | Speech and Sign

MANY HEARING PEOPLE who are unfamiliar with the signed languages of people who are deaf have difficulty conceiving of them, because of their radically different mode of transmission, as having the same communicative power as spoken languages. Thus Edward Tylor, an influential British anthropologist of the nineteenth century:

> It has to be noticed that the gesture-language by no means matches, sign for word, with our spoken language. One reason is that it has so little power of expressing abstract ideas. The deaf-mute can show particular ways of making things, such as building a wall or cutting out a coat, but it is quite beyond him to make one sign include what is common to all these, as we use the abstract term to "make."[1]

Tylor here remarks on the tendency of all known signed languages to be mimetic where possible or to make use, in Peirce's terminology, of "iconicity." Or more recently, the American psychologist Helmer Myklebust, presumed by many to have been an expert on the psychological functioning of deaf people:

> The manual language used by the deaf is an ideographic language. . . . it is more pictorial, less symbolic. . . . Ideographic language systems, in comparison with verbal symbol systems, lack precision, subtlety, and flexibility. It is likely that Man cannot achieve his ultimate potential through an Ideographic language. . . . The manual sign language must be viewed as inferior to the verbal as a language.[2]

The game of disparaging other people's languages in support of political positions has, of course, a long and disreputable history that begins at least with the Greeks, who saw no value in the languages of the barbarians (foreigners whose speech is represented by nonsense syllables—"baba"). Charles Darwin, otherwise one of the most astute observers of the natural world in recorded human history, had this to say about the "barbaric" inhabitants of Tierra del Fuego:

> The language of these people, according to our notions, scarcely deserves to be called articulate. Captain Cook has compared it to a man clearing his throat, but certainly no European ever cleared his throat with so many hoarse, guttural, and clicking sounds.[3]

Mark Twain raised this sport to high art in his burlesque of "the awful German language" in *A Tramp Abroad*. However, under the leadership of anthropological linguists such as Franz Boas and Edward Sapir in the early twentieth century, a dogma of equality of spoken languages took root in the scientific study of language. Here, for example, is Sapir's famous statement of the principle, in his 1921 classic, *Language:* "The lowliest South African Bushman speaks in the forms of a rich symbolic system that is in essence perfectly comparable to the speech of the cultivated Frenchman."[4] However, steps toward similar treatment of the signed languages of deaf people were not taken until the 1950s.

We have already noted that Western thinking about the signed languages of deaf people has oscillated between acceptance and rejection of their legitimacy. Here it might be worth considering some generalizations about how these languages were viewed by the intellectuals of the Enlightenment on the one hand and those of the Victorian era on the other. These generalizations are very broad but appear supportable. The first schools for deaf people, based upon instruction in sign language, arose during the European Enlightenment of the eighteenth century and appear to have flourished in an atmosphere of toleration, at least in France and the United States during the early part of the nineteenth century. The roots of American Sign Language, in fact, can be traced to the school for the deaf in Paris that was founded by the Abbé de l'Epée in 1755. The Victorian era of the mid-to-late-nine-teenth century, with its emphasis on moral and material progress, was quite another matter. During this latter period, the method of oralism came to dominate the education of deaf children through-out the Western world. According to the dogma of oralism, espe-cially as propounded by its archprophet, Alexander Graham Bell, sign language was a primitive form of communication that inter-fered with the struggle to teach deaf people to speak articulately and to speechread, and, as it was only by making them appear to be hearing that they could be "restored to society" to participate fully in social and economic life, signing had to be suppressed. Eugenic ideas about preventing marriages among deaf people also contributed to the desire to minimize socialization among them.[5] Oralism dominated the education of deaf children well into the middle of the twentieth century, and the passage from Myklebust quoted earlier may be considered typical of the majority opinion about sign language.

There should be little wonder then that the efforts to describe the signed languages of deaf people in linguistic terms following William Stokoe's pioneering work tended to focus on the similar-ities between sign and speech. Like any good anthropological lin-guist, Stokoe focused first on the visual analog in ASL of the sound systems (phonological systems) of spoken languages. His goal was to invent a descriptive system for the language that was based on linguistic principles (see fig. 13).[6] Realizing that he had to over-come the prejudices of an establishment of hearing professionals exemplified by Myklebust, Stokoe felt that these principles would have to mirror closely those that had been applied to spoken lan-guages. These principles included identification of at least the fol-lowing: sublexical structure and contrast at the sublexical level. Stokoe also realized that a fundamental difference exists between signed and spoken languages, something that other sign linguists have sometimes forgotten or ignored—the problem of simultane-ity in the presentation of various elements of signs. He described how this difference was overcome in the invention of descriptive

Fig. 13. William Stokoe (right) works with his colleague Carl Croneberg on the first ASL dictionary, ca. 1960, at Gallaudet University. Reprinted, by permission of the publisher, from *Seeing Language in Sign* by Jane Maher (Washington, D.C.: Gallaudet University Press, 1996), 40. Copyright 1996 by Gallaudet University.

elements he called "cheremes"—the visual-gestural analogs of phonemes:

> Signs cannot be performed one aspect at a time, as speakers can utter one segment of sound at a time. Signers can of course display handshapes of manual signs *ad libitum,* but they cannot demonstrate any significant sign action without using something to make that action somewhere. By an act of the imagination, however, it is possible to "look at" a sign *as if* one could see its action only or its active element only or its location only. In this way *three aspects* of a manual sign of sign language are distinguished, not by segmentation, it must be reemphasized, but by imagination.[7]

Stokoe's three aspects of a sign can be described as follows: (1) the place where it is made (the *tabula* or *tab*), (2) the distinctive configuration of the hand or hands making it (the *designator* or *dez*), and (3) the action of the hand or hands (the *signation* or *sig*).[8]

Note that this is a descriptive system for *manual* signs. Other gestures, such as facial ones, that are now recognized as part of the language are not as easily described by this system, but the system has stood the test of time and can still be usefully applied to the description of signed languages. It is easy to see how aspects of handshape—orientation, for example—could be described in terms similar to those of the distinctive features of speech sounds (see fig. 14 for the most frequently used ASL handshapes.)

Stokoe's success in winning acceptance of ASL as a natural human language, at least from the scientific community, is one of the great intellectual achievements in the behavioral sciences. A large number of language scholars are now working on ASL and other signed languages of people who are deaf, and the literature describing ASL may surpass that of most of the world's spoken languages. Moreover, as we saw above, light was shed on other issues in the study of language, including its evolution and questions about its very nature. However, this was not accomplished without some perhaps unintended intellectual costs, especially what could be described as the "procrustean bed" approach to describing ASL. Whatever aspects of signed languages seemed not to fit received notions about language had to be lopped off, and most especially the fundamental iconic or mimetic basis of a visual language had to be denied by sign linguists. This principle was seized upon by generations of scholars, including Tylor and Myklebust, who wanted to deny linguistic status to visual–gestural systems. What follows will mainly address the question of the significance of iconicity in signed languages.

In one sense, it is difficult to understand why hearing people like Tylor could not see past the iconicity. Surely, it is not particularly hard to imagine a visible sign for something that has no physical resemblance to the thing it refers to. Many things that human beings need to communicate about are abstract entities and require arbitrary signs (see fig. 15 for sample ASL handshapes). Although this example would not have been familiar to Tylor, any American who has watched a baseball game has seen the signals

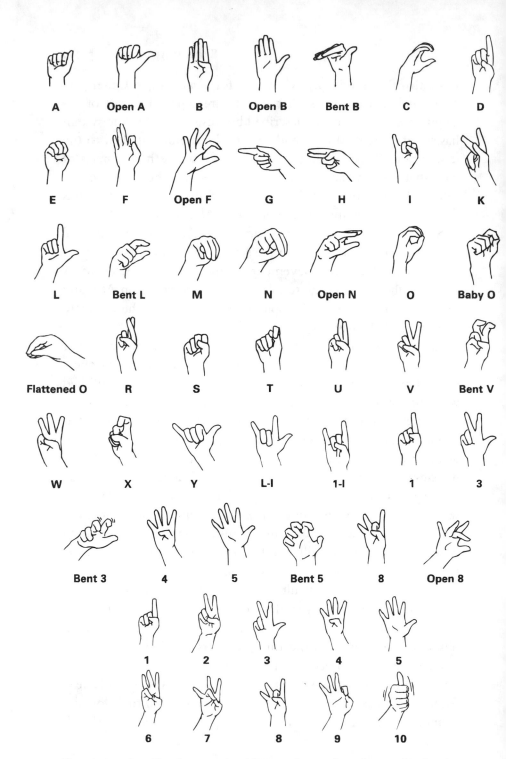

Fig. 14. American Sign Language handshapes and manual numbers used in forming signs. Reprinted, by permission of the publisher, from *The American Sign Language Handshape Dictionary* by Richard A. Tennant and Marianne Gluszak Brown (Washington, D.C.: Gallaudet University Press, 1998), 26, 28–29. Copyright 1998 by Gallaudet University.

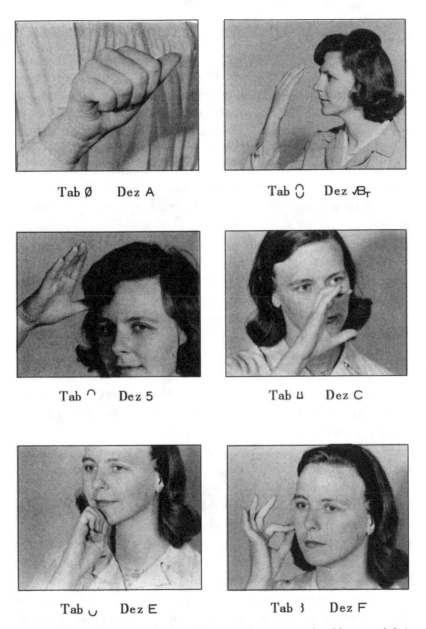

Tab Ø   Dez A   Tab Ͻ   Dez √B̞ᴛ

Tab ∩   Dez 5   Tab ⊔   Dez C

Tab ∪   Dez E   Tab Ʒ   Dez F

Fig. 15. One of William Stokoe's collaborators demonstrates handshapes and their locations for a variety of ASL signs. Reprinted, by permission of the publisher, from *Dictionary of American Sign Language* by William C. Stokoe, Dorothy Casterline, and Carl Croneberg (Washington, D.C.: Gallaudet College Press, 1965), xv.

that the third-base coach flashes to the batter. Not only are these entirely arbitrary and nontransparent, but meaningful signals are mixed with meaningless ones to confound the attempts of the opposing team to decode them. Signals of this sort are common in many activities that are conducted under noisy conditions or when silence is required. It should not have been surprising, therefore, that ASL would be found to have signs that are arbitrary and abstract as well as signs that are iconic and concrete. There is surely no way to adequately represent an entity like the U.S. Constitution iconically, but an arbitrary sign for it is easy to invent.

But prejudices die hard, and it was important for early linguistic treatments of ASL to establish that it did indeed have sufficient similarity to speech to be considered a full-fledged language. However, in addition to the ways in which signed languages are *like* spoken languages, they differ in equally interesting ways, and these differences deserve fuller treatment than they have received. To make the case for this, it would be instructive to resort again to the time-honored device of the thought experiment. Consider a world in which human evolution, having reached a crucial branching point, took a different path from that which led to today's spoken languages.

We have already considered the idea of a time in the history of the hominids during which linguistic communication was accomplished largely through visible signing instead of speech. Let us assume that the selective advantages that led to the predominance of speech weighed instead, for whatever reasons, in favor of signing, so that the norm for modern human linguistic communication became signed instead of spoken. Vocal communication would have continued to be used by hearing people, but only as an auxiliary gestural system for such purposes as attracting the attention of another signer or for indicating stress or emphasis during a signed performance. In this world, deaf people would be seen by hearing people as only mildly handicapped; they would be unable to use vocal gestures appropriately, and they would be unable to detect environmental sounds, but they would not require special educational methods and settings, and they would be able to socialize easily with hearing people. Deafness would scarcely be noticed or remarked upon. The people at greatest disadvantage in this world would be the blind ones, and for our purposes here they would be the most interesting as well. For centuries, all those people blind from birth or infancy would be considered incapable of communicating adequately with the sighted, except through a medium of crude tactile and oral gestures, incapable of learning to use that crowning achievement of human evolution, language, and so incapable of thought.

At some point during the Enlightenment a French cleric, having been asked to provide religious instruction to some blind children, would notice that they seemed to have an extensive set of oral or vocal gestures that they used to communicate among themselves. In a flash of inspiration, the Frenchman would realize that this native communication system could be used to form the basis of an educational system for blind children. Taking advantage of the existing stock of oral gestures, he would devise an extensive system of oral communication that mirrored in effectiveness, he would claim, the signed languages of the sighted majority. There would be skeptics. The American inventor of a televisual communication device would later claim that the Frenchman's system was crude and ineffective, that its use led to the social isolation of blind people, and that only a tactile version of signing could "restore" them to society. Those who were blind would argue that only their natural form of oral communication was truly effective in providing for their education and the establishment of a functioning social group.

Eventually a sighted researcher at the American University for the Blind would demonstrate, to the satisfaction of professional linguists, what the blind people had been maintaining all along, namely, that their oral communication system possessed the requisite characteristics to be considered a natural language. This would not end the debate or the political struggles. The proponents of the tactile system would compile a list of the deficiencies of the vocal system. The most damaging statement on these deficiencies would be published by a respected American psychologist and psychometrician:

> The oral language used by the blind is an Arbitrary language. . . . it is less pictorial, more symbolic. . . . Arbitrary language systems, in comparison with visual signed systems, lack precision, subtlety, and flexibility. It is likely that Man cannot achieve his ultimate potential through an Arbitrary language. . . . The oral language must be viewed as inferior to the visual language.

Particulars of this bill of attainder would include the following: oral languages would be found incapable of precisely indicating direction, shape, size, or myriad other physical characteristics of objects; they would be found deficient in exactness of pronomial reference; unnecessarily redundant; hopelessly prolix. It would be pointed out that they were made up primarily of a stock of elements unrelated in any meaningful way to the objects and actions they were meant to represent. It would be inconceivable to many observers that this language could possibly map onto the visible world in any very useful way. Psychologists would postulate that this language of sounds must result in an extremely impoverished mental life for blind people.

The purpose of this short excursion into an imaginary world is, of course, simply to illustrate that upon taking up a phenomenon as an object of study, people naturally notice first what is most salient about that phenomenon. In addition, members of our species will ascribe positive value to that which is characteristic of their own social group and will denigrate what is characteristic of others. Had linguistics been invented by signers instead of speakers, it seems likely that different conclusions would have been reached about the essential features of human languages. When the first speaking linguists began to contemplate their subject in the nineteenth century, they were most struck by what had struck Shakespeare in *Romeo and Juliet,* that no obvious resemblance existed between "a rose" and a rose, between words and the objects to which they referred. When systematic correspondences were identified between words and objects in different languages, it was taken as evidence of genetic relationship between the languages, not some fundamental characteristic of the correspondences. The linguists were next struck by the systematic ways in which certain sounds were used in some languages and not in others, and this observation led to the development of modern structural linguistics.

The untestable hypothesis being offered here is that signing linguists would have taken a different tack; they would have seen something else as salient. They would have noticed that across signed languages there were very often systematic correspondences between signs and their referents, but they would quickly have realized that these correspondences were not reliable indicators of genetic relatedness between languages. They would also have noticed systematic and unsystematic differences in classes of signs across languages. Their science of language would have had its basis in attempting to explain or predict when classes of signs could be expected to show systematic similarities and when they could be expected to show differences. They would have noticed, for example, that in most languages there would be signs referring to eating or food that involve movement of one or both hands toward the mouth. They would call this property of language *iconicity,* and they would postulate that iconicity is a necessary characteristic of human languages. They would also notice that many signs lacked this property, and they would develop rules to predict when signs could be expected to be iconic and when not.

However, in a linguistics based on spoken languages, iconicity is seen as somehow primitive, and it has been given short shrift by the scientific linguistics of signed languages. In fact, one could almost say there has been a taboo against discussing it.[9] This tendency emerged because Saussure and others declared that to be linguistic, signs (here in the inclusive semiotic sense) must be arbitrary—this even though iconicity is so clearly a fundamental organizing and creative force in signed languages. The American linguist Charles Hockett has described the underlying principle as *dimensionality:*

> The difference of dimensionality means that signages [Hockett's term for signed languages] can be iconic to an extent to which languages cannot; . . . while arbitrariness has its points, it also has its drawbacks, so that it is perhaps more revealing to put the differences the other way around, as a limitation of spoken languages. Indeed the dimensionality of signing is that of life itself, and it would be stupid not to resort to picturing, pantomiming, or pointing whenever convenient. . . . When a representation of some four-dimensional hunk of life has to be compressed into the single dimension of speech, most iconicity is necessarily squeezed out.[10]

It is worth noting that for hearing speakers not to make use of these devices as well, through the gestures accompanying their speech, would be stupid.

But let us look again at the hypothetical signed languages of our imaginary majority, had that evolutionary road been taken, and ask how they would come to be written. Presumably there would be much evolutionary agreement between signers and speakers, at least in the early stages. The first writing of signers would, in fact, be precisely like the first writing of speakers: it would consist of strings of pictured objects, which in the course of evolution would become increasingly stylized and associated with the phonology of the language. However, this writing system for sign language would not evolve into an alphabetic system—in its latest stages it might be something like the writing system of modern Chinese. Note here that, contrary to Professor Myklebust, an ideographic (actually logographic) writing system has proved adequate to the needs of the Chinese, one of the world's most complex societies, through many centuries.[11]

In attempting to assess the true value of those things that we currently consider important, it is sometimes instructive to listen to our intellectual ancestors. On the value of ideographic as opposed to alphabetic writing, Matteo Ricci, a Jesuit scholar of the sixteenth century and missionary to the Chinese, was unbiased.

According to Jonathan Spence, "Ricci, on first seeing Chinese ideographs in Macao in 1582, was to be . . . struck by their incredible potentiality for serving as universal forms that could transcend the differences in pronunciation that inhered in language."[12]

Because of their dimensionality, existing signed languages have resisted reduction to alphabetic writing. Despite almost forty years of the best efforts of linguists and others, those who write about American Sign Language still generally use pictographs to represent the signs they discuss. Because of the extreme complexity of the sublexical structuring of ASL (in four dimensions), reducing it to the two dimensions of phonetic writing may prove more trouble than it is worth, now that digitized video recording permits instant, accurate recording and retrieval of signed performances.

This standing of conventional linguistics on its head is not intended as an attack on the hard-won victories of sign language linguists in convincing the world that signed languages are really languages. However, certain properties of signed languages that make them unlike spoken languages are deserving of increasing attention, and this discussion of attempts to write ASL leads naturally to consideration of the nature of the sublexical structuring of signed languages.

As we have seen, one of the most salient characteristics of spoken languages is the lack of any apparent relationship between words and the things to which they refer—that is, they tend to be arbitrary or symbolic. Furthermore, words can be broken down into smaller particles that seem to have rules of assembly independent of the rules for assembling words into sentences. This property of spoken languages has been called duality of patterning or double articulation, and the question has frequently been asked whether signed languages can be said to have this property also—that is, whether it is a necessary property of language. To address this question, and the question of the evolutionary origin of duality, it is necessary first to discuss the elements of this duality.

The human vocal apparatus is capable of producing a large array of sounds. Each language incorporates a small and relatively fixed number of these, and the sets of sounds, so incorporated, differ from language to language. We discussed a definition of these sound classes or phonemes in the previous chapter. From the stock of phonemes are generated the smallest meaningful units, or morphemes, and from morphemes are created words, the smallest independent meaningful units. For example, in this system of classification, *ful* is a morpheme that could be incorporated into a word such as *meaningful*. Finally, words can be strung together to create sentences.

The rules in a given language for generating morphemes from the stock of phonemes (the phonological level) are independent of the rules for generating meaningful utterances (words and sentences—the syntactic level) from the stock of morphemes. This is a general statement of the principle of duality of patterning. For reasons that should become clear, these elements relating to duality of patterning imply that languages having this characteristic will tend to have arbitrary or symbolic relationships between words and the things to which they refer. Moreover, languages vary radically with respect to the elementary sound classes (phonemes) that they incorporate. For example, even the total number of phoneme classes may vary considerably, from perhaps as few as thirteen (Hawaiian) to perhaps eighty in some Caucasian languages.[13] This variability allows us easily to recognize some languages even when we don't know them, and for this reason we find nonsense mimicking of languages amusing. For instance, most of us instantly recognize the punchline to an old joke about an alleged Hawaiian fertility god—Kamanawanalaia. The fact that only a limited number of these phoneme classes exist in any spoken language is, of course, what makes alphabetic writing possible.

Closer examination of these elements suggests that the patterning in language is more than just dual, as the *phonological/syntactic* distinction implies. In fact, it is possible to identify at least four possible levels of patterning entailed by the foregoing description, levels that have been used for various purposes in structural linguistics:[14]

1. *Phonetic* level—This level pertains to the physical characteristics of the sounds that are employed by the speakers of a particular language (or all the sounds that could be employed); i.e., phonetics of a language or general phonetics.
2. *Phonological* level—This level pertains to the classes of sounds (phonemes), meaningless in themselves, that specify differences in meaning in that language, as well as the rules for assembling these phonemes into meaningful units (morphemes).
3. *Morphological* level—This level pertains to the rules of assembly of morphemes into independent, meaningful units (words).
4. *Syntactic* level—This level pertains to the rules for assembling words into higher order utterances (phrases and sentences).

Recalling again that the break we are concerned with here is that between the phonological and the morphological (between the meaning*less* and the meaning*ful*), it is appropriate to ask what we should look for if we want to demonstrate that a communication system, say a signed language, has the property of duality. The following criteria could be proposed as a test for duality of patterning in signed languages:

1. Selection by users of a particular signed language of a relatively small number of the handshapes, facial expressions, and so on that could be used to constitute minimally contrasting pairs. This stock of elements should be relatively fixed (i.e., the introduction of new elements or the deletion of old elements should occur only rarely).
2. Evidence of systematic rules for articulating these meaningless units into signs.
3. Evidence that the rules of articulation of the meaningless "phonological" items are independent from the semantic and syntactic constraints on the assembly of higher order utterances.

The argument for duality in American Sign Language is strongest from the first of these points, progressively weaker from the next two. First, it is not clear that the handshapes of ASL, usually thought of as elements in the stock of phonemes, are themselves always or even usually meaningless in isolation. This can be made clear by consideration of the C or cupped handshape when it represents cylindrical or spherical objects; or the F handshape (first finger opposed to thumb, other fingers extended) when it represents slender objects that can be grasped. In addition to having other handshapes that clearly resemble the objects to which they refer, ASL is also packed with mimetic movements of the hands, arms, and body. Whether these handshapes and movements are more comparable to morphemes or to phonemes, or whether they are sometimes one, sometimes the other, is not clear. Second, because of the fundamental iconicity underlying signing, it is also unclear if a strict separation exists between the levels with respect to rules of articulation, or if the rules are always fixed; that is, because of the gestural element in the language, rules may be relaxed on an ad hoc basis.

What one sees in ASL is a system that appears more open-ended in its ability to incorporate new signs but that has a tendency over time to compress these signs from pantomime or pictography into the formal system described by Stokoe. In some cases signs will never be so compressed. A good example of this is the sign for the number 4—made, of course, by simply holding up four fingers. It would be insane to make this sign any other way, and, in fact, it could be argued that this is not really an ASL sign at all, in that it is in general use among the hearing population of the United States and most of the rest of the world. Although the 4 handshape may be used in other signs, it is difficult to conceive of another handshape being used to make the sign for 4 (the only other remote possibility would be to hold up the thumb and first three fingers with the pinkie abducted), and, in this respect, the organization of ASL and other signed languages differs fundamentally from that of any spoken language. Theoretically and practically, we could find any set of phonemes in the repertoire of English being used for the word *four* and not be surprised; this statement would be equally true with respect to almost any English word. But such is simply not the case for a large proportion of the lexicon of ASL or other signed languages. The reason for this difference derives simply from the greater possibilities for iconic representation that visible languages afford. Incidentally, the counting system of English is not immune from iconic representation of a less direct sort: note that the smaller numbers in English are represented by words with few syllables, with progressive increase in the number of syllables as the represented numbers become larger.

To try to incorporate the handshapes of the ASL counting system into an abstract, formal phonology would likely be a mistake. The counting system in ASL has a logic all its own that has little to do with the rest of the language other than the first few numbers having an obvious iconicity. Counting in ASL, up to 100, is simply a progressively elaborated counting on the fingers. Above 100, the system (inherited from French methodical signs) incorporates the fingerspelled letters of the Roman numeral system: C for 100, M for 1,000. (The Roman numeral system, again, illustrates that all human languages will be iconic when they can—like the first few ASL numbers, the first three Roman numerals are simply completely representative marks on paper.) When ASL numbers correspond to other formal elements of the ASL phonological system, it is purely by coincidence—as in the correspondence between the number sign 9 and the F handshape. The F handshape happens to occur at the point in the sequence of finger-counting where the number 9 *must* be placed. It is also the case that the handshape for the number 7 (third finger opposed to the thumb, other fingers extended) occurs almost nowhere else in ASL. In other words, it is a special-purpose phoneme, functioning almost exclusively as a placeholder in the counting system. In this way, the counting system of ASL differs fundamentally from that of a spoken language like English. Again, the reason for this is simply the greater possibility for direct representation (of small numbers) in a visually expressed language.

The main point is this—signed languages remain open-ended in their ability to incorporate new signs that would not fit any phonological system we might devise for them; and while many lexical items, especially those that are hardest to express iconically, will have a tendency to be compressed into a fairly restricted phonological domain, others, such as those in the counting system, will be resistant to this sort of compression, especially when they are easily represented iconically.

Spoken languages, of course, also have this property, but to a much smaller degree. Take, for example, the utterance, "He went ****," where the asterisks represent the universally understood lip buzzing for breaking wind. This represents a perfectly good English sentence that is understandable to any native speaker. It happens that this sound (sometimes called "the raspberry") falls outside of the English phonological system as linguists have analyzed it; nevertheless, the utterance remains perfectly grammatical, understandable English. Moreover, utterances like this one are common in the ordinary discourse of hearing people. The difference in this regard between signed and spoken languages is one of degree and not of kind, but the difference in degree is significant, and it is probably true that sign language linguists have gone too far in stressing the similarities. So, to the extent that ASL exhibits something like duality of patterning, that duality will be less thoroughgoing than in spoken languages.

Margaret Deuchar has succinctly stated the position that what is important in language, signed as well as spoken, is not so much the arbitrariness of the sign, or its duality, but rather its conventionality:

> It may therefore be appropriate to redefine Saussure's principle as one of conventionality. Language would then be characterized as a system based on convention, or shared knowledge, among its users. This would shift the emphasis in defining language from properties that are assumed to be internal to it to properties as defined by its users, thus taking account of the social functions of language.[15]

Duality of patterning is thought by many linguists to be of fundamental importance in language, even a necessary characteristic; but it is hard to pin down why this should be. The most commonly invoked reason is that it allows for unlimited productivity in the creation of words and sentences. According to this argument the speaker need only know a small number of basic units and the rules for their assembly, so that from this knowledge a virtually infinite number of meaningful words, phrases, and sentences could be generated. This principle would work at both the phonological and syntactic levels. However, the speaker would still have to remember semantic correspondences for a large number of words. Or is the number really all that large for the average speaker?

Phonemicization of spoken languages makes possible alphabetic writing. As we have seen, many writing systems (Chinese, Classical Mayan, etc.) make relatively less use of systematic correspondences with the phonological system of the language in devising written symbols than is true of alphabets (see fig. 16). The fact that China could operate a successful bureaucracy and complicated economic system for thousands of years with a nonalphabetic writing system should alert us to the possibility that human

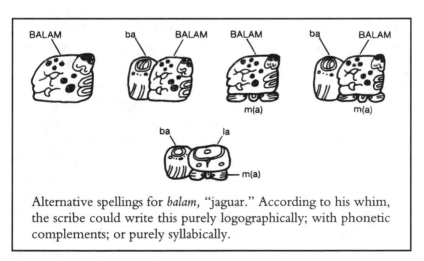

Alternative spellings for *balam,* "jaguar." According to his whim, the scribe could write this purely logographically; with phonetic complements; or purely syllabically.

Fig. 16 The Mayan writing system involved the use of logograms (some of which were quite iconic) to represent whole words or morphemes. Reprinted, by permission of the publisher, from *Breaking the Maya Code* by Michael Coe (New York: Thames and Hudson, 1992), fig. 67. Drawing by Michael Coe.

beings can communicate quite effectively through a system requiring the memorization of a large number of complex meaningful symbols with very complex substructures. A more convincing argument for the importance of phonemicization and duality can be made on the basis of the sensory system (hearing) involved in spoken language, and the neurological substrate supporting this system. According to Gordon Hewes:

> There is empirical evidence suggesting that our mental lexicons (we may have several different systems, differently organized) are in part accessible by means of a system remarkably like that which permits us to insert or retrieve items from an alphabetized file or dictionary.[16]

Here is an argument based on increased efficiency in storage, retrieval, and processing, not necessity. It is likely that different neurological constraints are placed on language in the visual channel.

Some scholars have argued that signed languages used by people who are deaf are not good test cases for how language might look in another sensory modality because they always coexist with dominant spoken languages and, therefore, are not called upon to carry the full weight of social intercourse within any extensive population. For example, many new lexical items in ASL seem to involve initialization, or the use of the fingerspelled first letter of the corresponding English word.[17] To understand this process, some understanding of the history of ASL is necessary. The process of formalization of the language began in France under the Abbé de l'Epée at the end of the eighteenth century, and its development was bound up with that of the one-hand manual alphabet. This system was imported into the United States early in the nineteenth century by Thomas H. Gallaudet and Laurent Clerc, a French teacher of deaf people who was himself deaf. Since that time, ASL has probably always been influenced by English—most adult deaf people in the United States attain some degree of literacy in the English language, and it would be strange if they did not take advantage of the vast lexical resources of English when the need arises to add items to their language. However, no compelling reason is apparent for believing that ASL could not take up the full weight of social intercourse in the absence of a dominant majority language like English. Certainly, new lexical items are introduced into ASL by means other than initialization (see chapter 6), and no apparent practical limit exists on the size of the ASL lexicon.

Even if we could perform the requisite naturalistic experiment, involving a deaf community that was completely isolated from the hearing world, there would still be a serious question about the evolutionary status of signed languages. Assuming that the structural studies of ASL have demonstrated that it is possible for a signed language in use among a modern human population to have some degree of duality of patterning, the question remains as to why this should be so. Deaf people who use ASL have modern human brains, and their ancestors were hearing, speaking people whose brains, in turn, evolved under whatever selective pressures were entailed in the process of the evolution of speech. The ability of modern deaf people to invent and use sophisticated signed languages may result from their ancestors having evolved as speakers. There is another quite plausible explanation, however.

The need to develop duality in spoken language may have been a primary driving force behind the evolution of human intellectual capabilities, as the Canadian linguist Edwin Pulleyblank has suggested.[18] But the capacity for inventing languages with duality of patterning in both the vocal and visual modes may be a special instance of a more general cognitive capacity. A reading of sociocultural theory, for example the "emics" and "etics" of Kenneth Pike,[19] suggests that culture in general must be considered to be complexly patterned and layered in ways that are not dissimilar from those found in the more restricted domain of language. Whether the need to develop duality in an auditory mode was the evolutionary driving force behind all of this remains an open question, but it seems likely that something much more general was happening.

The preceding arguments lead to some very general suggestions about the nature of the earliest linguistic units that will be more thoroughly explored in the next chapter. The usual evolutionary sequence is to think of simple, phonemelike elements coming first and then being elaborated into words and finally sentences, but it may be the other way around. It may be that the earliest linguistic units were large and semantically complex—sentencelike rather than wordlike—and primate vocalizations could provide a possible model for them. The idea that primate vocalization systems might be precursors of human language has been proposed and attacked on several occasions. It is not necessary to enter into this debate in depth here. Suffice it to say that plausible objections to the possibility of continuity between chimpanzee-like vocalizations and human speech have been raised on both neurological and anatomical grounds. Plausible arguments for continuity have also been proposed, and common sense would suggest that, given the volubility of chimpanzees in the wild, a "mute" stage in the evolution of the hominids is unlikely. What is being proposed here is simply that human use of manual gestures provides an even better model for how this process might have occurred than does vocalization.

Notes

1. Tylor ([1881] 1965, 30). ASL, and quite likely the British sign language that Tylor observed, has a perfectly good sign for the abstract concept "make."

2. Myklebust (1957, 241–42) and see Padden and Humphries (1988, 59).

3. Darwin ([1845] 1937, 210f).

4. Sapir (1921, 22).

5. See Winefield (1987); Baynton (1996).

6. Stokoe (1965).

7. Stokoe (1980).

8. Stokoe (1965).

9. Wilcox (1996).

10. Hockett (1978, 274).

11. The term *ideographic,* is much used and much misunderstood.

Technically, it means a sign that represents an idea—and this would be true of any linguistic sign or symbol, including words. As applied to writing systems like the Chinese system, the term *ideogram,* generally means a character that represents the concept to which a word refers without necessarily representing the sounds that express the word in speech. In this way, such a system is quite different from a phonetic system. Most linguists, however, prefer the term *logographic,* to refer to systems like the Chinese, because the Chinese characters actually represent Chinese words or morphemes, without necessarily representing their sounds. It is for this reason that some Chinese characters can be used to write words with similar meanings in other languages, as they are used for this purpose in Japan, for example. The Chinese writing system also involves phonetic markers and markers that specify the class of objects to which a character refers. Western scholars have long characterized Chinese logographic writing as somehow inferior to or more primitive than alphabetic writing (see Coe, 1992). It was this prejudice that Myklebust was drawing on in dismissing sign language as "ideographic."

12. Spence (1984, 21).
13. See, for example, Pulleyblank (1986).
14. For example, Harris (1993, 29–30).
15. Deuchar (1985, 242).
16. Hewes (1983, 72).
17. Pulleyblank (1986).
18. Ibid.
19. Pike (1956).

4 | Words and Sentences

TO MANY PEOPLE, it seems easy to conceive of the origin of words, but where on Earth do sentences come from? Most of the scholars who have written seriously on the subject of the origin of language agree that the sentence-forming, or syntactic, capacity of human language is what separates it from all other animal communication systems. Chimpanzees are clearly capable of learning and using appropriately a large number of signs, whether indexic, iconic, or symbolic; but there seems to be a severe limitation on their ability to combine these signs, in novel ways, in strings that are more than two or three items long. This problem seems especially intractable from the Chomskyan perspective, so much so that Derek Bickerton suggests that a special mutation is required to allow human beings to create syntactic systems. In his view, a communication system either has syntax or it doesn't—there are no intermediate stages.[1]

Syntax is, indeed, held in such high regard that the biologist John Maynard Smith gives it special treatment in his book *The Major Transitions in Evolution*. He is quite impressed with Bickerton's argument but stops short of accepting the need to invoke a special mutation to make it possible. Maynard Smith, as an evolutionary biologist might be expected to do, speculates that there must be intermediate stages between communication systems—like the artificial ones used experimentally with chimps—that do not seem to have syntax, and human languages that do.[2] Some dissenting voices with respect to this rampant syntaxophilia have emerged. For example, Terrence Deacon has recently provided a refreshing antidote by proposing that, in fact, grammar is not all that hard to evolve.[3] Instead Deacon argues, as we will see in chapter 6, that symbolic reference was the real bottleneck through which hominids had to pass.

Bickerton's point of view can be understood when syntax is seen as a closed system that involves the mapping of a hierarchical mental structure onto a linear structure of arbitrary sounds in the creation of a linguistic utterance and vice versa in its apprehension. This mapping is usually conceived in terms of tree diagrams branching at appropriate nodes of logical bifurcation. According to the contemporary American philosopher, Willard Van Orman Quine, in a critique of the Chomskyan system:

> The trees used to be mere *ad hoc* scaffolding by the aid of which the grammarians, each in his own way, contrived to specify the objective totality of well-formed sentences. According to the new doctrine, the trees are themselves part of the objective linguistic reality to be specified.[4]

If there is any caveat that a scientist should be aware of, it is that just because a theory "explains" the phenomenon under study it is not necessarily a good representation of reality. Theories of cosmology prior to Copernicus and Kepler fairly accurately described and predicted the motions of the planets in terms of intricately interlocked circular orbits around the earth. This system was based on the notions that the earth was at the center of the universe, that the most perfect curved path was a circle, and that surely God would not create something as important as the movement of the planets along less-than-perfect lines. Reality turned out to be simpler and more elegant. Copernicus showed that the planets, including the earth, revolved around the sun, and Kepler, through painstaking analysis, showed that the orbits were really elliptical. A generation later, Newton provided an explanation for this sort of orbital motion through a theory called gravitation.

Curiously enough, it was a reaction by William Stokoe to what he saw as an increasingly unjustified proliferation of abstractions in the field he created that led him to a second fundamental contribution to the science of language and to a solution to this seemingly intractable problem—how syntax might have arisen in evolutionary terms. Never one to suffer fools gladly, Stokoe expressed his objections to developments in *sign phonology* in very vivid terms in 1991:

> Sign phonology can be as complicated as anyone wants to make it; in this respect it differs not at all from phonology generally. As evidence for this I cite a review in the international newsletter *Signpost* of a book that gets to the bottom, says its reviewer, "of autosegmental, metrical, and also lexical phonology." Once highly regarded (by philosophers at least) as a safeguard against unnecessary overelaboration, Ockham's Razor and even the computer programmer's vernacular KISS (Keep It Simple, Stupid) seem to have been forgotten in recent treatments of phonology—treatments that are almost, I am tempted to say, independent of language, certainly of language as laymen use it.[5]

The problem of unnecessary complication may be endemic to linguistics. Even Steven Pinker, the great explicator of Chomskyan theory, recognizes similar problems of obscurantism at work in generative grammar theory in his book *The Language Instinct*. Pinker bemoans this as leading to a lack of recognition of the underlying elegance of the theory.[6]

With respect to the problem he raised, Stokoe proposed a simple solution:

> What I propose is not complicated at all; it is dead simple to begin with. I call it semantic phonology. It invites one to look at a sign— i.e., a word of a primary sign language—as simply a marriage of a noun and a verb. In semantic terminology, appropriate here, the sign is an *agent-verb* construction. The agent is so called because it is what acts (in signing as in generative semantics), and the verb is what the agent does. What could be simpler?[7]

According to Stokoe, it is thus unnecessary to invoke even the phonological aspects of signs that he had proposed in his original "cherological" description. This new system, moreover, welcomes clearly iconic and mimetic signs into its fold. In fact, it is the application of semantic phonology to the study of iconic visual-gestural signs that leads to proposals about the origin of *syntax*.

Working with his colleagues, Sherman Wilcox and the author of this book, Stokoe has attempted to show how semantic phonology can be applied to the problem of the origin of syntax.[8] It should be stated at the outset, however, that semantic phonology has been poorly understood by some linguists because it directly challenges the notion of separate levels presented in the preceding two chapters. In particular, it seems to contradict the most basic dogma of structural linguistics, that of duality of patterning by combining the phonological with the semantic. Stokoe is saying, in effect, that the smallest elements of the descriptive system are themselves meaningful, and that, moreover, they have distinctly grammatical functions—that is, they *act* like nouns and verbs. Bruce Richman suggests that what Stokoe does here is clear-cutting:

> This view of language as all surface and no depth, local phenomenon with proliferating, horizontal offshoots going in all directions at once as *rhizomes* do—with no deep processes, no derivational "trees"—is the great alternative . . . suggested by Stokoe in his recent work on "semantic phonology." Stokoe suggests that the "phonology" (i.e., distinctive movements) and semantics of sign language gestures are produced and given meaning in one *Moebius strip* movement: the phonology and semantics being just different ways of looking at the same, *one* movement.[9]

Here Richman refers to an aspect of Chomskyan theory that specifies three components to a grammar: a syntactic component, a semantic component, and a phonological component. According to Chomsky, for each sentence there is a "deep structure" specified by the syntactic component. This determines its semantic interpretation. The syntactic component also specifies a "surface structure" that determines the sentence's phonetic interpretation.[10] As we will see later, other, more conventional linguists find Stokoe's flattening of the hierarchy very disquieting—partly because what is implied is simultaneous processing, as opposed to more serial, hierarchical parsing.

To understand how syntax might have arisen, one must consider the application of semantic phonology to the special case of iconic manual signs. The reader is invited to make the sign for "grasp" or "capture" by moving the active hand (the right in most people), with the fingers extended, toward the upraised index finger of the other hand, the fingers of the active hand finally closing around this index finger. Stokoe invites us to see in this action the seed of syntax. The active hand is at once the agent (subject) of a simple sentence, the moving hand is the verb, and the index finger is quite literally the "direct" object of a transitive verb—the active hand actually makes contact with it.

This sign itself can be seen to exhibit both simultaneous and sequential elements. The active hand has to start somewhere, move, and end somewhere, yet both hands are in the field of vision together during the entire time that the sign is being executed. Moreover, signs like this can be combined, and one can be inserted between two others, while "hierarchical" relations among them, including subordination, may be indicated simultaneously by actions of other parts of the body, such as the face. It is not such a tremendous leap from this to the elementary syntax of a human language.

Perhaps even more apropos is another example that would generally be considered an ASL sentence consisting of three signs, and glossed into English as VEHICLE GO-AROUND PERSON, or translated into English as, "The car goes around the person." This sentence is described in figure 17 according to Stokoe's notation from his *Dictionary of American Sign Language* (DASL),[11] semantic phonology (signs), and syntactically (S[ubject] V[erb] O[bject]). According to the description given, this sentence consists of one hand in the 3 handshape moving around the upright index finger of the other hand. The motion is continuous and both hands, with their given shapes, are again continuously in the field of vision of the interlocutors. But how can we segment this sentence into its

gloss	VEHICLE	GO-AROUND	PERSON
syntax	S	V	O
signs	noun (verb)	verb (noun)	noun (verb)
DASL notation[a]	3	<	G^

Description: Unrotated forearm with thumb and first two fingers extended moves (upper arm extension, slight inward rotation and wrist bending) past and around upright index finger of other hand.

Fig. 17. Four ways of writing a simple ASL sentence. Adapted from *Gesture and the Nature of Language* by David F. Armstrong, William C. Stokoe, and Sherman E. Wilcox, (Cambridge: Cambridge University Press, 1995), 15.

constituent signs? The "verb" glossed as GO-AROUND is simply the continuous action, given as (<) in Stokoe's cherological notation, of the 3 hand. Note that had the 3 hand made contact with the upright index finger of the other hand, the meaning of the sentence would be greatly altered to a message about the tragic fate of a hapless pedestrian.

Commenting on an extended version of this model presented by Armstrong, Stokoe, and Wilcox in their book *Gesture and the Nature of Language,* the linguist Mike Beakan fails to grasp its significance. Beakan is troubled by two things about this model: that it fails to separate the syntactic from the semantic, and that it fails to take into account "the significance of action."[12] But clearly Stokoe's original intent was to experiment by purposely blurring the boundaries between levels, as Richman understands, and, even more clearly, this is an action-based model. It attempts to build syntax from the simultaneous and sequential actions of hominid bodies in motion. This theoretical position assumes that the selective value that inheres in language has to do with increments in fitness to those who are able to use it to organize productive group activities. It also assumes that increased fitness accrues to those who can store and retrieve information about the social group and its environment in the course of face-to-face interaction.

To understand what is at stake here, one must consider the more specific claims that have been made about the nature of syntax in the literature of Chomskyan linguistics. Currently, the clearest statement of these claims is contained in Steven Pinker's popular recent book, *The Language Instinct*. Pinker here gives an eminently straightforward and readable account of the central claims of the Chomskyan school. Pinker begins his account with the familiar statement of the uniqueness of language: it is a system that allows human beings to create and apprehend a virtually infinite number of meaningful utterances, thereby enabling them to exchange information about anything under the sun (and some things that aren't). This, in turn is made possible by two "tricks":

> The first principle, articulated by the Swiss linguist Ferdinand de Saussure, is "the arbitrariness of the sign," the wholly conventional pairing of a sound with a meaning. . . . The second trick is captured in a phrase from Wilhelm Von Humboldt that presaged Chomsky: language "makes infinite use of finite media." We know the difference between the forgettable *Dog bites man* and the newsworthy *Man bites dog* because of the order in which *dog, man,* and *bites* are combined. . . . [W]e use a code to translate between orders of words and combinations of thoughts. That code, or set of rules, is called a generative grammar. . . . The principle underlying grammar is unusual in the natural world. A grammar is an example of a "discrete combinatorial system." A finite number of discrete elements (in this case words) are sampled, combined, and permuted to create larger structures (in this case sentences) with properties that are quite distinct from those of their elements.[13]

It should be clear by now that all of the claims made in this passage from *The Language Instinct* are under dispute in this book: arbitrariness, finiteness, and discreteness of linguistic elements can all be criticized from the perspective of signed languages. That these claims may be accurate with respect to speech is, perhaps, arguable, and, in fact, speech is all that Pinker is attempting to explain: "Grammar is a protocol that has to interconnect the ear, the mouth, and the mind, three very different kinds of machine.

It cannot be tailored to any of them but must have an abstract logic of its own."[14]

So what is the nature of that logic? The claims at the center of the Chomskyan program are that this logic is hierarchical and modular, and that it cannot be acquired in its entirety by a growing child simply through associative learning. The latter claim implies that, to some extent, the rules of grammar are "hardwired" into the brains of all human beings—that they are genetically determined. Two principal kinds of evidence are usually adduced in support of this determinacy claim: what has been called the "poverty of stimuli" in the environment of the growing child; and a point made at least as early as the seventeenth century by Descartes that, regarding human beings, "there are none so depraved and stupid, without even excepting idiots, that they cannot arrange different words together, forming of them a statement by which they make known their thoughts."[15] Thus, no child is exposed to even a fraction of the potentially infinite number of well-formed sentences that are possible in his or her language, yet each child eventually acquires the ability to produce and recognize grammatical sentences to which he or she has never been exposed; and even people with significant mental deficiencies are able to speak grammatically.

With respect to the hierarchical and modular claims, several types of evidence are generally adduced, and, again, Pinker's presentation of this evidence is so clear and straightforward that it will be summarized here. First, evidence suggests that grammatical sentences are not formed simply on the basis of probabilities of association, as simple word chains, one of the possible approaches that human beings could take as a strategy in sentence formation. Pinker provides a famous example from Chomsky of what appears to be a "grammatical" sentence that apparently has a zero probability of actually being uttered in ordinary English discourse: "Colorless green ideas sleep furiously."[16] We will visit this sentence again when we consider the question of how meaning is established, but it is frequently given as an example of the independence of the grammatical rules of English from any necessity to produce meaningful sentences. This argument depends upon the acceptance of this sentence as having proper grammatical form by most speakers of English and of its being meaningless.

If grammatical relations among words are not established by some sort of simple probability table, how are they established? In general, the solution suggested by Chomsky draws upon the familiar concept of parts of speech but uses these concepts in a new and more powerful way. The most fundamental property of language to be addressed is the seeming ability of speakers to produce a potentially infinite number of sentences, a problem that can be solved by specifying a set of recursive rules—*recursion* being a mathematical term describing formulas that generate successive terms of a function by a set of rules applied to preceding terms. In language, according to Chomsky, recursion is achieved by a set of rules called a "phrase structure grammar." Grammaticality, according to this theory, depends critically upon the sorting of words and phrases by their function, at its most basic level into nouns and verbs or noun phrases and verb phrases.

Again, according to Pinker:

> The difference between the artificial combinatorial system we see in word-chain devices and the natural one we see in the human brain is summed up in a line from the Joyce Kilmer poem: "Only God can make a tree." A sentence is not a chain but a tree. In a human grammar, words are grouped into phrases, like twigs joined in a branch. The phrase is given a name—a mental symbol—and little phrases can be joined into bigger ones.[17]

Pinker uses a simple example to illustrate the reasoning that is at the heart of Chomskyan theory—simple rewrite rules are the basis for the syntactic system of any language. Pinker asks the reader to consider the following English sentence: "The happy boy eats ice cream." This sentence consists of two phrases: "The happy boy" and "eats ice cream"—a noun phrase (NP) and a verb phrase (VP). In fact, English sentences can be defined minimally as noun phrases followed by verb phrases. The verb phrase, in turn, consists of a verb and a second, subordinated noun phrase: "ice cream." The sentence can be diagrammed as a simple inverted tree, as shown in figure 18.[18]

This way of diagramming the structure of the sentence reveals two fundamental features of the Chomskyan system—its modularity and its ability to account for the embedding of subordinate elements, in this case the embedding of a second noun phrase—*ice cream*. Embedding is a fundamental feature of human languages that is difficult to explain through simple word-chain models. This second noun phrase could be extended ad libitum, for example: "the delicious rum raisin ice cream with butterscotch topping." The second feature that is revealed, modularity, is defined thus by Pinker: "The key insight is that a tree is *modular,* like telephone jacks or garden hose couplers. A symbol like 'NP' is like a connector or fitting of a certain shape. It allows one component (a phrase) to snap into any of several positions inside other components (larger phrases)."[19]

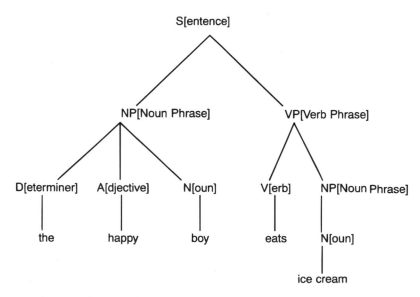

Fig. 18. Tree diagram of a simple sentence. Adapted from a diagram in Pinker, *Language Instinct.*

This manner of describing syntactic processes becomes increasingly complex, but it is not necessary to explore more of its details here—suffice it to say that it has proved extremely powerful as an analytic tool and has led to fundamental insights about the structure underlying all human languages. However, it is equally important to consider what is left out by this model, especially when presented as a model of how the human brain actually works, and when the purpose is to explain how human beings might have acquired the ability to perform the functions that the model implies. Chomsky himself and his followers have generally avoided this latter question. Although he seems to be implying that a Supreme Being might have been involved ("Only God can make a tree"), Pinker, unlike Chomsky, has at least attempted to provide such an explanation in terms of Darwinian principles.

First, let us consider what is left out. In effect, what is denied by this model is a significant role for inductive reasoning in the acquisition and use of language. What this model implies, most fundamentally, is that the brain contains lists of words that belong to certain categories, and that selections from these lists ("representations") are then combined according to a very limited set of specified rules. So, if words necessarily belong to particular categories, ambiguities can arise when a word might belong to more than one category. For example, consider this example of a hypothetical newspaper headline: TEACHER STRIKES IDLE CHILDREN. We find this amusing because the word *strikes* might belong either to the noun phrase or the verb phrase, and a critical difference in meaning depends on its membership. Chomskyan theory claims to help us understand how this ambiguity arises. But if language has the neat, logical properties suggested by Chomskyan theory, why would there be ambiguous words such as these that *could* belong to more than one category? The most parsimonious answer is that languages are not divine creations—they have histories, and sometimes they need to be ambiguous. Human beings have always lived with uncertainty and have had to reason inferentially using probabilistic assumptions. In ordinary speech, a statement such as this would easily be disambiguated either by context or by appropriate stress applied by the person uttering it.

In fact, human political processes would be impossible without a communication system that allowed for substantial ambiguity yet was clear enough to facilitate social action. When Henry II said, "Who will rid me of this meddlesome priest?" was he merely expressing, by way of a rhetorical question, his irritation with the uncooperative behavior of an old friend, or was he issuing an execution order to his trusted knights? Either way, Thomas à Becket was soon dead, and the king, although perhaps with ambivalence, had accomplished an important political objective while retaining enough deniability, following some acts of atonement, to survive the wrath of Church and people.[20]

Although frequently denied, there is an accompanying assumption in formal linguistics that people ordinarily communicate in the sort of convoluted sentences that grammarians love to analyze. Experience, however, tells us that the more usual human interchange is something like the following fictional example of a transaction in a coffee shop, inspired by Erving Goffman:[21]

> Waitress: Coffee?
> Customer: Please.
> Waitress: Black?
> Customer: Cream and sugar.
> Waitress: Be right back.

One piece of evidence adduced in support of the modularity hypothesis is that use of language is "automatic" and requires no thought—that language is something like a reflexive (instinctive) response. That belief is probably correct with respect to the sort of formulaic interchange presented above. However, most readers will not find automatic their comprehension of the following, highly embedded sentence from Kant's *Metaphysic of Morals*:

> A good will is good not because of what it performs or effects, not by its aptness for the attainment of some proposed end, but simply by virtue of the volition—that is, it is good in itself, and considered

by itself is to be esteemed much higher than all that can be brought about by it in favor of any inclination, nay, even of the sum-total of all inclinations.[22]

Conjuring up a mental tree might help us puzzle out what Kant, writing through a translator, is trying to tell us here, but such trees are unlikely to be used by most people very often. It is a common experience for most people that a complex sentence may have to be repeated before it is understood, and for mistakes in production and apprehension to increase directly with the complexity. In fact, sentences like this are meant to be *read* and not *heard*. They become "parsable" only through the luxury of time for backtracking that literacy affords.

Something like this difference between Kant and the coffee shop appears to be what Basil Bernstein had in mind when he called attention to types of language use that he termed "elaborated" and "restricted codes."[23] In a restricted code, there is no expectation that significant "new" information will be exchanged; instead, ordinary social processes are maintained by it, and there is a heavy reliance on the kind of formulaic expressions that were used by the coffee shop interlocutors. In an elaborated code, information exchange of a more formal nature takes place—new utterances are invented and less reliance is placed on nonverbal and metalinguistic events. In this scenario a grammar capable of producing an infinite number of new sentences might become indispensable.

A second argument often given in support of the modular hypothesis is the universal grounding of language, the similarities in terms of organization at the phonological and the syntactic level that are shared by all languages, and that presumably result from a genetically based Universal Grammar (UG).[24] According to Armstrong, Stokoe, and Wilcox:

> The fundamental problem with a "universal grammar" can be stated most simply as a hoary anthropological conundrum: "How many ways are there to make an oar?" Are the similarities among languages due to an innate genetically determined "grammar

organ" or . . . are they due to natural constraints imposed by human perceptual, cognitive and motor limitations and the need for language to "work"?[25]

To put this another way, should any sort of pancultural similarity in human behavior be taken as evidence for specific genetic determination? Because all human beings, for much of their evolutionary history, used similar stone tools, should we postulate a stone tool gene? Because all human societies developed origin myths, should we postulate an origin myth gene? Because the development of urban societies follows certain predictable sequences in terms of the introduction of priestly, warrior, and worker castes, should we postulate an urban civilization gene? For that matter, how about a warfare gene? Or a pyramid-building gene?

A better suggestion comes from consideration of what is actually known about the evolution of the primate brain and its accompanying behavior. The whole history of this development is away from genetic determination for specific behaviors (instincts) and toward the flexibility and adaptability of the individual within a social context. The regularity in human behavior across cultures seems much more likely to be the expression of powerful, but general, cognitive abilities being applied to similar problems that are found to have limited numbers of optimal solutions following generations of invention and experimentation. Languages can be viewed similarly within this framework of invention and experimentation. As we saw in chapter 1, Terrence Deacon extends this argument in terms of coevolution or Baldwinian evolution involving language itself and its biological substrates. According to this argument, any genetic changes that have occurred are seen as the result of genetic adaptation to the *use* of language (and in Deacon's argument language means speech), rather than being seen as somehow enabling language to exist at all.[26]

What actually is the evidence for genetic causation of specific aspects of grammar, and why is this issue important at all? First, it is necessary to point out that the issue is *all important* in the context of Darwinian approaches to evolution. Natural selection can act only on differences among individuals that have a genetic basis—according to the current dogma of evolutionary biology it cannot act on acquired characteristics. At some level genetic determination for the human ability to construct and use languages must exist, but that determination could be as general as the genetic program for large brain size. Language might simply be a property of a big brain, as Chomsky has pointed out.[27] What is at issue is whether the ability to construct and use syntax in a certain way is specifically determined. If this is the case, then the genes determining it should behave like all other genes and should exhibit variability due to mutation. It is that variability in the genetic makeup of individuals upon which natural selection acts. Until very recently, no genetic abnormalities affecting only some aspect of grammatical competence had been reported in the literature. As we will see in the next chapter, many instances of the entire syntactic process being wiped out by brain damage from stroke or accident were reported, but proponents of the genetically based modular hypothesis needed an example of something more specific being affected, as there are explanations for localization of functions in the brain other than specific genetic determination for grammar.

A genetically based grammar disorder has recently been described by Myrna Gopnick and widely interpreted as a "specific language impairment" (SLI). To qualify fully as revealing the action of a "grammar gene," this disorder would have to be just as the name implies—"specific." That is, it should clearly be a genetic disorder and it should affect only some aspect of grammatical processing. Gopnick's work, based on pedigree analysis and testing of individuals from a single family, appears to reveal simple dominant genetic causation for a disorder affecting family members' ability to use some of the inflection markers of English and nothing else.[28] As might be expected, the data and subsequent interpretations of SLI have been hotly contested. Pinker cites them as evidence of genetic determination for human syntax.[29]

Others who have done research on SLI-affected individuals have pointed out that it is not as "specific" as claimed, and that it affects articulation, general cognitive functioning, and, perhaps, the ability to process acoustic, phonological input.[30] The location of this gene has now been mapped onto human chromosome 7.[31] Suffice it to say that the issue is far from being settled and that the evidence so far adduced in support of the genetically based modular hypothesis is far from convincing.

In support of the modularity of language, claims have also been made that signed languages (actually ASL, the only signed language that has been studied sufficiently to support such a claim) have substructuring that is virtually identical to that claimed for spoken languages. In language that anyone who has taught profoundly deaf students will find familiar, Dorothy Bishop, a language acquisition researcher, questions this assumption: "[O]n tests of grammatical comprehension of English, there were many deaf children who had great difficulty in understanding the significance of contrasts signaled by morphological endings, function words and word order, regardless of whether or not they were perceptually salient."[32] Bishop goes on to report the following:

> Even those children with facility in a native sign language had major difficulties in decoding the syntax of English—presumably because the surface forms used in oral languages to mark grammatical functions (e.g., word order and morphological endings) are not well-suited to processing in the visual modality, where simultaneous rather than sequential grammatical processes are the rule. Thus hearing loss did not simply lead to slowing of language acquisition, nor did it lead to a predictable pattern of grammatical impairment affecting only non-salient morphemes. In fact, the distinctive response patterns seen in hearing impaired children were remarkably similar to those seen in hearing children who had been diagnosed as having receptive language disorders.[33]

It is especially important to note that Bishop is not simply regurgitating oralist diatribes against sign language use by deaf students—the problem is not being blamed on the "ideographic" nature of sign language. Instead, in addition to problems introduced by delayed onset of language acquisition, the issue really may be related to the way that the brain processes linguistic material presented in different modalities, an issue that will be explored in more depth in the next chapter. The problem for deaf students trying to become literate in a spoken language is to learn through deliberate instruction, rather than natural acquisition, the transformation of linguistic information from primarily simultaneous to primarily sequential presentation. This may also be the evolutionary path that was followed by the species during the course of its acquisition of speech.

If God, or a sudden macromutation, did not give us our ability to grow syntactic trees, how else might they have been planted? Unlike Bickerton, Pinker accepts the possibility of intermediate stages between simple, nonsyntactic communication systems and fully recursive human languages.[34] But what would these intermediate stages look like? Although he argues that natural selection could have acted upon genetically determined intermediates, Pinker does not offer many details. This may be because he does not see a role for visual–gestural systems in this history.

Stokoe's ideas about semantic phonology offer a possible answer that is more convincing than that offered by Pinker. First, it allows for a process through which nouns and verbs, as natural constituents of iconic gesture, could occur first as real human actions, rather than abstract concepts. These conceptual categories are the sine qua non of phrase structure grammar and must have come from somewhere. Stokoe offers a starting point that does not require a hypothetical, special mutation affecting brain structure. Second, we can see the roots of recursiveness, embedding, in the simultaneous subordinating activities of parts of the body other than the hands and arms.

Think for a minute about the cognitive operations that embedding seems to imply, and use the following example: "I can start, but not finish, this sentence." Here the phrase "but not finish" has been embedded within "I can start this sentence." This would seem to involve the ability of both the speaker and the hearer to hold in memory the first part of the sentence "I can start" until the arrival of the noun phrase that completes it: "this sentence." At the same time, both speaker and hearer must deal with the intervening phrase: "but not finish." This appears to be a complex task, and acquiring the ability to perform it seems to pose a substantial obstacle in evolutionary terms. In fact, what may be involved here is not so much remembering a logical relationship and then applying it, as simply being able to recognize and then attend to a set of overlapping relationships. If we think back to what is involved in dealing with a sign (sentence) like VEHICLE GO-AROUND PERSON, we may begin to recognize the roots of this ability. Here again, all the elements of the sign were simultaneously in the visual field of both the signer and the viewer as the action unfolded, and both had to be able to decode this complex set of elements as the action revealed the relationships among them. The ability to maintain attention to a complex, changing pattern could be the key to understanding this simple sign/sentence, as it could also be the key to understanding an embedded phrase.

Finally, and perhaps most important, semantic phonology allows us to deal with the lingering feeling that everything is not as clear-cut, not as either/or, not as binary as Chomskyan linguistics would suggest. If languages are really governed by sets of simple yet powerful rules for generating all of their sentences, why has the problem of machine translation proven so intractable? Several answers emerge. First, the rules are not that all-encompassing. The English language, for example, appears to be partly systematic and partly cobbled together from whatever was available in the historic word bin. In Sapir's terms: "Unfortunately, or luckily, no language is tyrannically consistent. All grammars leak."[35] In a 1991 article in the journal *Science,* Pinker suggests that what underlies English is part modular system and part simply rote learning.[36] His examples have to do with the past tense, which involves many verbs that follow a regular rule in the formation of their past tenses, as well as some notoriously irregular verbs, including *to be,* for which there is nothing like a rule. The verb *to be,* of course, is not God-given—it has a history, its paradigm having been derived from three different Indo-European roots.

Second, the elements may not be all that discrete—here, fuzzy logic may help us. A second example from Pinker's article, presented in defense of the modular argument, helps, in fact, to undermine it. As evidence of the strength of the past tense rule and of the reality of the nominal and verbal categories, he cites the manner in which the past tense is applied to certain nouns that have come to be used as verbs. These nouns all have elements that resemble irregular verbs and his examples include the following: "one says *grandstanded* not *grandstood; flied out* in baseball [from a fly ball] not *flew out; high-sticked* in hockey, not *high-stuck.*" In discussing these examples, Armstrong, Stokoe, and Wilcox point out that the situation is not as clear-cut as Pinker suggests.[37] Although they would opt for the regular past tense in these cases, they contend that most English speakers would not feel entirely comfortable with it for these verbalized nouns. In fact, it is relatively easy to avoid using it. For example, one can use the past progressive— *he was grandstanding*—to avoid having to use the simple past tense. Although these words have not yet become real verbs, we can understand what they are in terms of fuzzy logical prototypes— they are as yet only partly verbs and that is why we feel awkward applying to them operations that are reserved for true verbs. Here, then, are induction and probabilistic inference at work. Furthermore, although this possibility has been denied by Chomskyan linguists, plausible computer models of language acquisition have been developed that employ probabilistic, inductive learning strategies, so-called "neural networks," to arrive at the acquisition of fully recursive language.[38]

If we see spoken languages developing at least partly out of signed languages, in the manner proposed by Stokoe, it is possible to see why we can handle both categorical and fuzzy logical sorts of mental operations. Several things are clear about visible gestures. Although they can involve binary contrast, as in the difference between specific handshapes, there is no limit on the number of elementary gestures that can be performed, as there *is* a limit on the number of ways that the vocal tract can be configured to produce speech sounds. In indicating direction or location, for example, one can point anywhere. For this reason construction of a sign language phonology that exactly mirrors phonologies of spoken languages has proved impossible—the potential "phonological" spaces of signed languages simply cannot be segmented in the same way. So, signed languages do not operate on a finite set of elements—they have potentially infinite resources. As Stokoe suggests with respect to semantic phonology, their categories are not as discrete as those of spoken languages—a noun of ASL may imply a microstructure composed of nounlike and verblike elements. Again, the system described by Pinker may be simply what is needed to make speech work, given the severe constraints placed on human beings in producing and apprehending sound. This necessarily means that speech appears abstract to us, and it requires that our spoken words generally be arbitrary symbols rather than iconic or indexic. The higher order cognitive functions needed to make it all work together may have evolved during the course of human use of communication systems employing both visible and vocal gestures over millennia.

So rather than postulating a mutation that inserted trees into the brain as an explanation for how human beings came to be able to handle hierarchical logical structures, let us instead consider how human beings were able to handle multiple-channel simultaneous gestures, because this surely is how we have communicated since the beginning of the hominid line. Given what we know about the material culture and anatomy of *Homo erectus,* members of that species seem likely to have had the capacity to communicate gesturally using the sort of simple semantic phonological sentences that have been discussed here. When we narrowly define language as speech, we lose the valuable insights that a broader view gives us into our past and our origins.

Notes

1. Bickerton (1990).
2. Smith and Szathmáry (1995, 279–309).
3. Deacon (1997).
4. Quine (1974, 105).
5. Stokoe (1991, 107).
6. Pinker (1994, 104–5). A desire for simplicity may have been at least part of the motivation for Chomsky's (1995) introduction of the "minimalist program."
7. Stokoe (1991, 107).
8. Armstrong, Stokoe, and Wilcox (1995).
9. Richman (1997, 27).
10. Chomsky (1965, 16).
11. Stokoe (1965).
12. Beakan (1996, 66).
13. Pinker (1994, 83–84).
14. Ibid. (125).
15. See Chomsky (1966, 4).
16. Pinker (1994, 88).
17. Ibid. (97–98).
18. Ibid. (99).
19. Ibid. (99).
20. There have been many versions of this story, including plays by Jean Anouilh and T.S. Eliot.
21. See Goffman (1971).
22. Tillman, Berofsky, and O'Connor (1967, 294).
23. Bernstein (1964, 259–60).
24. We have already reviewed some of these similarities in this and the previous chapter. Following is a summary of this evidence from Pinker (1994, 237–38):

Chomsky's claim that from a Martian's-eye view all humans speak a single language is based on the discovery that the same symbol-manipulating machinery, without exception, underlies the world's languages. Linguists have long known that the basic design features of language are found everywhere. Many were documented in 1960 by the non-Chomskyan linguist C. F. Hockett in a comparison between human languages and animal communication systems (Hockett was not acquainted with Martian). Languages use the mouth-to-ear channel as long as the users have intact hearing (manual and facial gestures, of course, are the substitute channel used by the deaf). A common grammatical code, neutral between production and comprehension, allows speakers to produce any linguistic message they can understand, and vice versa. Words have stable meanings, linked to them by arbitrary convention. Speech sounds are treated discontinuously; a sound that is acoustically halfway between *bat* and *pat* does not mean something halfway between batting and patting. Languages can convey meanings that are abstract and remote in time or space from the speaker. Linguistic forms are infinite in number, because they are created by a discrete combinatorial system. Languages all show a duality of patterning in which one rule system is used to order phonemes within morphemes, independent of meaning, and another is used to order morphemes within words and phrases, specifying their meaning.

Pinker goes on to list more grammatical universals that have been discovered through the application of Chomskyan analyses.

25. Armstrong, Stokoe, and Wilcox (1995, 122).
26. Deacon (1997).
27. See Pinker (1994, 362–63).
28. Gopnick (1990).
29. Pinker (1991).
30. Bishop (1997).
31. Fisher et al. (1998).
32. Bishop (1997, 2). The document cited was retrieved from World Wide Web site http://www.chass.utoronto.ca :8080/epc/srb/srb/7-2edit.html.
33. Ibid. (2–3).
34. Pinker (1994).
35. Sapir (1921, 38).
36. Pinker (1991).
37. Armstrong, Stokoe, and Wilcox (1995, 134–37).
38. See Deacon (1997, 130–34) for a summary of this evidence.

5 | Simultaneity and Sequentiality

SHOULD A CLEAR difference between spoken and signed languages exist with respect to the relative salience of simultaneous and sequential processes, and if speech and visible gesture have coexisted for millennia, then contrastive study of the two systems should shed light on the nature of language itself. To many of us, speech appears quintessentially sequentially organized, while signing seems especially packed with elements that appear simultaneously. As we have seen, this difference arises as a result of differences in human sensory capacities in the auditory and visual modalities. Human beings simply have a much greater capacity to obtain information through the visual channel than they do through the auditory, so the auditory channel seems constricted. In the first chapter information was provided on evolutionary trends in the Primates, including the trend toward elaboration of the sense of vision and of the brain in general. Here we will consider whether the human ability to deal linguistically with simultaneous and sequential processes may have been enabled by neurological specialization at a very gross level, that of the two cerebral hemispheres. For the reader to follow the argument that is presented in the remainder of this chapter, it is necessary to consider further some general aspects of the architecture and function of the human brain.

Le Gros Clark summarizes the most important trends in the evolution of the primate brain, traits that are most fully expressed among humans.

> Undoubtedly the most distinctive trait of the Primates, wherein this order contrasts with all other mammalian orders in its evolutionary history, is the tendency towards the development of a brain

which is large in proportion to the total body weight, and which is particularly characterized by a relatively extensive and often richly convoluted cerebral cortex. It is true that during the first half of the Tertiary epoch of geological time the brain also underwent a progressive expansion in many other evolving groups of mammals, but in the Primates this expansion began earlier, proceeded more rapidly, and ultimately advanced much further.[1]

The sheer increase in the brain-to-body ratio among the hominids and possible functional reorganization of the major components of the brain were surely important in the evolution of the human capacity for language. Here we will be most concerned with the cerebral cortex, the so-called "gray matter," which covers most of the external surface of the human brain. Among the Primates, human beings have the largest amount of their brain composed of the cerebral cortex in both absolute and relative terms. In the evolutionary history of the vertebrate brain, older structures have generally been overlain by historically more recent structures, and the major trend among the Primates has been a reduction in the part of the forebrain concerned with the sense of smell and the great enlargement of the cerebral hemispheres and their outer cortex. In general, this cortex is involved in the processing of sensory input in the visual, auditory, and somatosensory channels, and with the control of motor output that becomes increasingly complex. Most of the neural pathways entering and leaving the cortex cross to the opposite side, so that the left cerebral cortex deals with the right side of the body, and vice versa.

The cerebral hemispheres are divided into several major lobes—the frontal, parietal, temporal, and occipital (see fig. 19). These, in turn, have been shown to have functional specializations (see fig. 20). At the most general level the frontal lobe, the expansion of which is most obvious among the hominids, is involved in the initiation of voluntary movement and in the planning and control of complex behavioral sequences. Control centers for various parts of the body are laid out in a generally consistent manner along the so-called "motor cortex" of the frontal lobe, and this

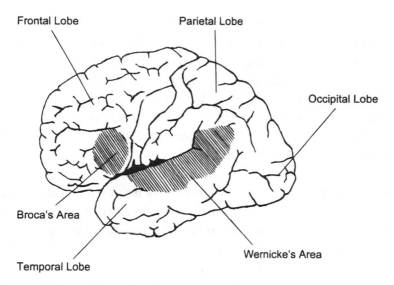

Fig. 19. Left hemisphere of the human cerebrum. Redrawn by Robert C. Johnson from a drawing in Lieberman, *Uniquely Human.*

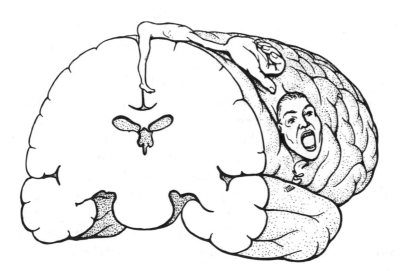

Fig. 20. The motor homunculus. Reprinted, with permission of the publisher, from *Human Neuroanatomy* by Raymond Truex and Malcolm Carpenter, 6th ed. (Baltimore: Williams and Wilkins, 1969). © Williams and Wilkins, 1969.

organization is frequently represented in terms of a "motor homunculus." In a book about the role that manual signing may have played in the evolution of the capacity for language, it would be strange not to comment on the prominence of the representation of the hand in the motor homunculus—it gets almost equal billing with the face and throat. The other major lobes are involved primarily in the processing and association of sensory input—this is especially true of the occipital lobe with respect to vision. Centers for auditory input tend to be located in the temporal lobe, and centers for somatosensory input tend to be located in the parietal cortex. Evidence for integration of sensory input across modalities in the inferior part of the parietal lobe also exists. This is a vast oversimplification of the functions of the cerebral cortex, but it should enable the reader to understand the argument that follows.

A central problem in the study of the evolution of the biological capacity for language has been to explain how the brain could deal with both the simultaneous and sequential aspects of language production and apprehension. Although speech and sign differ with respect to the relative importance of simultaneous and sequential functions, it is also true that both systems, to some extent, employ both kinds of functions. Early neurological studies, based almost entirely on the study of spoken language deficits following brain trauma, tended to focus either on the primarily sequential assembly processes of grammar and syntax, or on comprehension deficits—the model here being one of word "retrieval," again generally conceived of as a sequential look-up process, as from a mental dictionary or lexicon. This early work tended to locate the centers of language activity in the left frontal and temporal cortex of the cerebrum. This view of the neurological compartmentalization of language endures in the names of the cortical areas supposed to generate and comprehend language, Broca's and Wernicke's areas respectively, after the most notable of the nineteenth-century neurologists. Thus, Broca's area in the frontal cortex has been associated with grammatical or production functions of language, especially speech production, and Wernicke's area in the temporal cortex with its reception and decoding. As a result of this early work, there is an enduring view of the left hemisphere as the dominant or language hemisphere, and the right as the minor or nonverbal hemisphere.

The great French academic Paul Broca is particularly interesting in this context and it is worth discussing his views on sign language in a short digression. He is generally considered to be a founder of both neurology and physical anthropology, but at a time (1861) when signed languages were generally not held in high esteem either within anthropology or by society in general, Broca provided a definition of language that included sign:

> There are, in effect, several types of language. Any system of signs permitting the expression of ideas in a manner that is more or less intelligible, more or less complete, and more or less rapid, is a language in the most general sense of the word: thus speech, mimicry [that is, sign language], dactylology, figurative writing, phonetic writing, etc., are all types of language.[2]

Ironically, the great discoverer of the brain's speech center had allowed sign language into the linguistic tent as well.

The early part of the twentieth century saw an all-out attack on the "localization" view of language representation, coincident with, but not coincidental to, the rise of behaviorism. At mid-century, again coincident with the return, with a vengeance, of Cartesianism to linguistics, we saw the return of locationism to neurological perspectives on language, with interconnected left hemisphere "modules" seen as controlling aspects of language use, modules being understood to mean something analogous to plug-in electronic components or compartmentalized computational subroutines, or perhaps even the couplings of garden hoses, rather than the sort of vaguely isomorphic representation suggested by behaviorist or associationist theory. Much of the research of the 1960s and 1970s was performed on so-called "split-brain" patients, people whose cerebral hemispheres had been disconnected by severing the cerebral commissures as treatment for neurological ailments. These studies continued to reinforce the notion that the left hemisphere was the language hemisphere, but important functions for the right hemisphere also began to be identified, including facial recognition and visuospatial cognition. Finally, and most recently, a variety of neurological approaches, including electroencephalogram (EEG) and electrical stimulation studies, positron-emission tomography (PET), magnetic resonance imaging (MRI), and computer-enhanced methods that dynamically measure regional cerebral blood flow (CBF) have contributed direct information about the "real-time" functioning of the intact human brain.[3] In this chapter we will consider evidence supporting the view that the lateralization of the brain is not into a language (left) hemisphere and a nonverbal (right) hemisphere, but into two functional neurolinguistic units—one, the left, concerned primarily with sequential processes, especially acoustic processing; and the other, the right, concerned primarily with simultaneous aspects of language use, especially visual processing.

What then are the sequential processes of spoken language and how can it be said to employ simultaneous processes as well? To reiterate, first and most obvious among the sequential processes of speech is the activation of the vocal articulators in the production of a stream of speech—archetypically the function of Broca's area in the left frontal lobe. Recall, however, that in Jakobson's conception of phonology, phonemes can be seen as simultaneous bundles of distinctive features. From a neurological point of view, this can be put in terms of simultaneous firings of neurons involved in "packages" of articulatory "gestures" that are then arranged in sequence to produce a speech stream. Similarly sequential in nature would be the classic look-up functions of Wernicke's area. However, even here classic structural linguistics would suggest a combination of simultaneous and sequential processes in terms of what Saussure characterized as paradigmatic and syntagmatic functions.[4] Paradigmatic functions would be, as the name suggests, those involving the "selection" of the appropriate form of a word from, for example, the mental representation of its inflectional paradigm—the paradigm thus being seen as a simultaneous representation of all the possible forms of that word. Syntagmatic functions would be simply the well-known syntactic control of sentence assembly, a sequential process whereby the selections from the relevant paradigms are plugged into the appropriate slots in a sentence. This conception of the formation of the sentence can be seen as a forerunner of Chomsky's generative grammar.

Other simultaneous processes in speech are perhaps less obvious and more controversial from a neurological perspective, and contrary to the brief history of the study of cerebral lateralization given above, a careful review reveals a long history in the neurological literature of recognition of the involvement of the right hemisphere in language use. Several studies published in the 1960s and 1970s presented results concerning the extent to which the right hemisphere is involved in linguistic processes. According to a research report from the early 1960s:

> We believe that in general the results support the observation that in an adult population right cerebral damage is associated with linguistic and intellectual modification. Our impression is that the modifications tend to become more apparent as the linguistic tasks call for abstract concepts and require that the individual adjust himself to an established linguistic formulation.[5]

Other studies had shown that injury to the right hemisphere is associated with increases in latency for naming uncommon objects and with reductions in the ability to integrate a set of words, that is, to comprehend the relationships among words.[6] In 1973 the neurologist Joseph Bogen summarized numerous important findings concerning right hemisphere linguistic abilities, the most relevant of which follow:

> First of all, the aphasic [that is, a speech-deficient patient with left hemisphere trauma] often utters words or sentences. In fact, as Head pointed out: "When an aphasic cannot employ more abstract terms, he often uses descriptive phrases, similes, and metaphorical expressions in an appropriate manner."

Second, injuries to the right hemisphere produce certain defects in language or verbal ability. . . .

Third, a gross defect in understanding speech usually requires, in addition to a left hemisphere lesion, an associated deconnection of the right temporal lobe. . . .

Fifth, certain kinds of verbal activity (poetry) may first appear subsequent to an aphasiogenic left hemisphere lesion.

Sixth, vocalization as well as alteration of ongoing speech, have been produced by stimulation of the right hemisphere.

Seventh, the right hemisphere of the split-brain patient can read many words as well as understand spoken utterances.

Lastly, two adults having left hemispherectomy could each speak at least a few words; and a third could articulate long sentences while singing.[7]

With findings like these in mind, Stuart Dimond in the early 1970s proposed a model of cerebral hemispheric involvement in language use (see fig. 21).[8] Dimond hypothesized that linguistic processes prior to the actual motor output system could occur in either cerebral hemisphere. This hypothesis appears to be an over-simplified representation of what must be an intricate and reciprocal flow of information, but it serves to remind us that as long as a

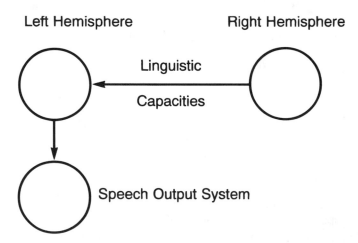

Fig. 21. Simplified diagram of cerebral hemispheric involvement in language processing. Redrawn from a diagram in Dimond, *Double Brain,* 176.

quarter century ago, neurologists had begun to see the processing of language in the brain as more complex than a simple modular explanation would imply.

More recently, descriptions assigned to linguistic processes appearing to have right hemisphere involvement include "connotative" as opposed to denotative processes, as well as metaphorical and "context" dependent processes.[9] A variety of neuropsychological studies, especially those of Howard Gardner and his associates, have focused on the role of the right hemisphere in the use of metaphor, verbal humor, and the "apprehension of complex linguistic materials,"[10] and it could be hypothesized that one of the functions of metaphor and other figures of speech is to "visualize" the acoustic symbols of speech for an animal whose primary sensory system is vision, a question that will be explored further in the next chapter.

A word of caution is in order here. The popular imagination was very much captured by the split-brain research of the past three decades, especially by the idea that human beings might, in effect, have two separate consciousnesses, centered in the two cerebral hemispheres. The left brain, with its ordering tendencies, came off as somewhat fascistic in this popular conception, while the right brain was seen as wild, creative, and mystical—a sort of dope-smoking, hippie artist. As a result of all this, many neurologists have become wary of any attribution of separate functions to the hemispheres. One does not want to overemphasize the holistic functions of the right hemisphere—we don't want to be, so to speak, "drawing from the right side of the brain" (after the title of a best-selling book[11])—but there does seem to be something real here.

Doreen Kimura, a pioneering Canadian neuroscientist and thoroughgoing empiricist, reassessed the clinical evidence for hemispheric control of language functions in 1993. Her work and that of others would seem to confirm the notion that the left hemisphere in most people is specialized for control of the motor pathways leading to speech, but she disputes the notion of clearly defined aphasias that differ depending on the part of the left hemisphere affected by trauma. Further, according to her assessment, the data on right hemisphere linguistic capabilities would seem to support some sharing of central conceptual control for language.[12] One should recall here that superiority has been shown for the left hemisphere in processing serially ordered perceptual input and for the right hemisphere in the treatment of perceptual "gestalts" or complex chunks of input. Remembering what has just been said about right hemispheric linguistic capabilities, a crude analogy could be made between Chomsky's phonological and syntactic components and left hemisphere function and between certain aspects of the semantic component and right hemisphere function. This analogy would of course be too crude, and it is certainly no longer supportable to argue that these components are in any sense independent.

Should we consider even this general level of localization of function to be indicative of specific genetic control for aspects of language? A consideration of the general topology of the human brain suggests not. Broca's and Wernicke's areas are located in or near the left anterior quadrant of the cerebral cortex, adjacent to the sensory and motor processing centers associated with hearing and vocalization. The general placement of these centers is similar among the higher primates, and this seems a sufficient explanation for the regular placement of speech centers at this location. No special genetic mechanism would thus seem to be required other than that controlling the general lateralization of neurological functions. In fact, research results published in 1998 indicate that chimpanzees have an enlargement in the left hemisphere of an area called the *planum temporale,* a region of the temporal lobe usually included in Wernicke's area in humans.[13] In human beings, this area is also generally larger in the left hemisphere than in the right. But so far we have been discussing aspects only of spoken language and their neurological control. Let us now consider the curious case of signed languages.

Serious study of the neurolinguistics of signed languages began soon after research conducted by William Stokoe and others was accepted as establishing the linguistic nature of the signed languages of deaf people. In laying the groundwork for linguistic study of signed languages, Stokoe insisted from the beginning that elements corresponding to the sequentially produced phonemes of spoken languages could be presented simultaneously in signs.[14] As we have seen, Charles Hockett has referred to this aspect of signed languages as "dimensionality."[15] Given evidence that the right cerebral hemisphere was heavily implicated in visual cognition and in "simultaneous" processing generally, it was initially supposed in neurolinguistic research on signers that heavy dependence on right hemisphere processing would be found. On the other hand was the expectation that, if they were really languages, signed languages should depend upon left hemisphere processing, much like spoken languages.

Studies have, in fact, been contradictory on this issue. Initially, traditional studies of brain-damaged signers (conducted by a number of researchers including Doreen Kimura[16]) showed aphasia-like deficits following left hemisphere damage, especially in brain regions usually associated with Broca's area in hearing speakers; but even as early as the late 1970s some studies indicated right hemisphere involvement in sign recognition.[17] Newer research methods, including CBF, applied to normally signing deaf individuals have revealed strong right hemisphere involvement in aspects of sign language use, especially sign recognition and especially with respect to the parieto-occipital area.[18] In this regard the history of neurolinguistic study of signed language has not differed vastly from that of speech, and following her review of the relevant studies, Kimura comes to conclusions about the neurological substrates of signed languages that are similar to her conclusions about speech. That is, that the motor control functions in both speech and signing are located in left hemisphere centers in or near the major motor control centers pictured in the motor homunculus. Other more general, especially "semantic" functions appear to have right hemisphere involvement. Kimura concludes that what links the motor output systems of speech and signing to left hemisphere structures is the need for "praxic" control—that is, control of the organization of complex behavioral sequences.[19] The unusually heavy loading of sign language processing in the right hemisphere, especially the parieto-occipital area, is most likely a consequence of its reception in the visual mode, and its exploitation of three-dimensional visual space.

An even more direct functional relationship exists between the lateralized functions of handedness (i.e., hand preference) and language. Kimura notes that manual signing and gesturing are skilled activities in which hand preference plays a key role.[20] In this regard it is significant that John Bonvillian, a psychologist at the University of Virginia, provides evidence that, among children learning ASL as a first language, hand preference appears in signing before it does in object manipulation.[21] This original preference is strongly correlated with the hand that eventually becomes the child's dominant hand—for example, eventual right-handers show strong initial preferences for using the right hand in early signing. If signing developed early in the hominid lineage as a principal means of communication, it becomes relatively simple to see an evolving neurological connection, at the level of cerebral laterality, between language and handedness. This would help to solve an enduring problem in understanding the evolution of the human nervous system: why are both handedness and aspects of language generally lateralized to the same, left, hemisphere?

Sherman Wilcox has pointed out that signed language linguistics has shared a symbiotic political relationship with the Cartesian (Chomskyan) linguistics of spoken languages.[22] To enhance the political status of signed languages as genuine languages, signed language linguists may have overemphasized some of the characteristics, such as arbitrariness of the sign vehicle, that signed languages share only partly with spoken languages. At the same time, Cartesian linguistics has embraced the notion of language in a modality other than the vocal as indicative of the existence of a disembodied language organ. This, Wilcox argues, has led to the adoption of some truly paradoxical positions concerning the nature of signed languages, and ultimately, of language in general. First is the idea that the "gestural" signs of signed languages, despite their resemblance to the gestures used by hearing speakers, could not have these gestures as one of their sources. That is, according to the standard dogma of linguistics, signed languages must be nongestural, helping to support a Platonic view of signing as necessarily independent of speech. This position, strongly held by many advocates of the use of signing in the education of deaf children, obscures a very real neurological connection between speech and gesture that leads to a final point about simultaneity in language and its neural control. This position mirrors, moreover, the dominant position taken in the traditional linguistics of spoken languages—namely, that speech is independent of the manual and other visible gestures that ordinarily accompany it. These gestures are seen as having a metalinguistic and nonreferential role in communication.

During the 1990s a number of scholars, including David McNeill, Adam Kendon, and Brenda Farnell, have expanded our understanding of the communicative function of visible gesture, and, in particular, the habitual use by human beings of coordinated streams of speech and visible gesture in the normal course of social interaction.[23] Moreover, neurolinguistic research increasingly indicates that speech and visible gesture are directed by a unified central control system, possibly located in the supplementary motor area of the left frontal lobe of the cerebrum.[24] Although debate surrounds the nature of this control system—that is, whether it is primarily a motor output system or a central symbolic system—this unity of speech and manual gesture suggests the evolutionary importance of this aspect of simultaneity in language. As has already been suggested, the most parsimonious model of language evolution would be one that posits the simultaneous use of both the acoustic and visual channels throughout the course of hominid evolution, with visible gesture probably taking the lead early in this history.

A simple example will serve to illustrate the interdependence of speech and visible gesture. Imagine that someone asks you how big the fish was that got away, and you respond in speech as follows: "About that big." That spoken response conveys no information other than acknowledgment that you apparently heard and understood your interlocutor. However, your spoken response is accompanied by rotation at your wrists so that your hands are held up in front of your chest with the palms facing each other. How far your hands are held apart depends on how big a liar you are. This is the way in which most people would answer this question, and clearly information about the size of the fish is not contained in the spoken utterance. You could also respond by saying "HUGE," with stress on the vowel, while simultaneously going up on tiptoe and fully extending your arms to each side. To call the spoken parts of these utterances language, and the visible gestures something else, seriously distorts the nature of how we habitually communicate.

There are a variety of reasons to believe that human beings have evolved capacities for language in both channels, and parsimony is served by supposing that those evolved simultaneously. We have already seen a neurological basis for this belief. An abundance of evidence further indicates that under the appropriate circumstances, human beings construct languages in either or both of these channels. Language is possible, of course, with no contribution from the visual channel—the telephone is a daily reminder of this fact—and the signed languages of profoundly deaf people similarly indicate that languages can operate fully without sound. In a variety of situations, however, frequently those involving interactions among deaf and hearing people, a dual-channel approach may be most effective.

Here it would be useful to introduce the unwanted and much-maligned stepchild of deaf education, a method known as "Simultaneous Communication" or "SimCom." SimCom involves an attempt to speak and sign the same message at the same time. In actual practice, what usually happens is that the sender of a SimCom message speaks in more or less complete English sentences and signs the verbs and nouns of these sentences, but not many of the "grammatical" words and affixes. The deaf interlocutor is usually dependent upon speechreading and context to supply the missing signed elements of the sentence.[25] If nothing else, Simultaneous Communication represents the extreme in what has been called "bimodal communication," communication involving some combination of manual/gestural signing and speech.[26] In Simultaneous Communication, both channels are supposed to carry the same referential content, and the method demonstrates the limits of the human capacity to perform in this way. SimCom was long considered artificial, "invented" for educational purposes, but it may not be. Something like it has been reported in use by hearing Plains Indian signers,[27] and by hearing and deaf users of an autochthonous sign language formerly used on the island of Martha's Vineyard.

The case of the deaf population of Martha's Vineyard is particularly revealing because the societal adaptation to it may be more typical of what generally happens in traditional societies than the "disability" model so often employed by the urban, industrial society to which most of us are accustomed. Nora Groce discovered that because of what geneticists call the "founder effect," there had been a high proportion of deaf people among the English-speaking inhabitants of the island for much of the seventeenth, eighteenth, and nineteenth centuries.[28] Because the population of the island was small and inbred during this period, the high level of deafness, introduced by the original English settlers, was maintained. By the time Groce arrived to do her research during the 1970s, this deaf population was only a memory, the recessive gene for deafness having been swamped by the huge influx of new residents that followed the Vineyard's conversion from a traditional society of farmers, fishermen, and whalers to a vacation and resort center in the twentieth century. What Groce was able to piece together about the traditional society's response to its deaf people is fascinating. Groce was able to show that because so many people on the island were deaf, and so many hearing people were related to deaf people, virtually everyone, hearing and deaf, could communicate in the sign language that developed there. So the deaf people, instead of being marginalized, participated in all aspects of social life. A small, closed society such as that could not afford to do otherwise, and similar responses to high levels of hereditary deafness in traditional societies have been reported among the Yucatec Maya of Mexico,[29] and on the island of Bali.[30] Groce provides the following quotation from a man who was in his late eighties at the time she was collecting data:

> We would sit around and wait for the mail to come in and just talk. And the deaf would be there, everyone would be there. And they were part of the crowd, and they were accepted. They were fishermen and farmers and everything else. And they wanted to find out the news just as much as the rest of us. And oftentimes people would tell stories and make signs at the same time so everyone could follow him together. Of course, sometimes, if there were more deaf than hearing there, everyone would speak sign language—just to be polite you know.[31]

Evidence from a variety of sources points to a common and simultaneous evolutionary history of speech and manual gesture. Under a purely Cartesian view, systems like SimCom should be impossible. Claims have, in fact, been made that SimCom, in the sense of simultaneous production of spoken English and ASL, *is* impossible.[32] The grammars and lexicons of the underlying systems are radically dissimilar, and the melding of the two should cause "interference." In the sense of the description of its use given above, however, SimCom is employed satisfactorily on a daily basis by many deaf and hearing people at places like Gallaudet University. In terms simply of its functional capacity then, SimCom can operate much like a natural language in satisfying the normal communication needs of its users.

Carol Padden offers interesting counterpoint to the political controversy that has surrounded the use of SimCom in the education of deaf students in the United States. As was indicated above, claims have been made that speech and sign *could* not be used together. There have also been political claims that they *should* not be used together. This may result from aspects of the linguistic culture in the English-speaking world that go beyond the world of deafness and deaf education. Padden points out that when Italian deaf people sign with one another, they use what appears to an American observer to be a high proportion of mouthed Italian words, where an American would fingerspell English words. According to Padden, this appears "oral" to many American deaf people, while the American practice of fingerspelling with little lip movement is characterized by Italian deaf people as appearing "mute." In Italian sign language, the mouthed Italian word functions as the visible sign, a practice that very rarely occurs among American deaf signers. Padden concludes that there needs to be more consideration given to such "non-pure" systems. Perhaps part of the explanation for the difference lies in what most speakers of English would view as the greater penetration of spoken Italian by visible gesture than is true of most spoken English. It may simply be that Italians, both hearing and deaf, see less of a separation between the two systems than Americans do. The traditional explanation for this phenomenon, among deaf Italians, is that spoken Italian is unusually easy to speechread.[33]

If something like SimCom is possible, does this constitute further evidence against the modular view of language? Or is a modular view reinforced? As an alternative to a specific modular view, we can follow Merlin Donald and reconsider the old idea of an "homuncular" central executive in the brain, in this case as an aspect of the working memory system.[34] Although Donald does not claim any biological reality for such a central executive and he ultimately concludes that it is not sufficient, we could speculate that such a system could involve the inferior parietal lobe and the frontal supplementary motor area of the left hemisphere. The input and output systems, as well as the longer term memory traces for the grammars of multiple language systems, could still be represented in more or less "isomorphic" associationist neural loci elsewhere in either hemisphere of the brain. The central system

Fig. 22. Kalahari
hunting signs.

SECRETARY BIRD

SCRUB HARE

Hunting in pairs, Bushmen chatter with each other a great deal, but once an animal is sighted or its spoor picked up, they stalk in silence, using signals to keep each other informed. Most often these identify an animal by its most salient feature. Thus, upheld arms and outstretched index fingers suggest big horns—as seen in the picture for the greater kudu (*this page, 3rd row, right*). In the signal for giraffe (*this page, 4th row, left*), however, it is not the giraffe's long neck that is being mimicked but its head, with the spread, slightly curling fingers representing the ears and stubby horns; this distinguishes it from the signal for ostrich (*opposite page, top row, right*), in which an arm forms the bird's neck. When an animal defies description, the signal may be an animated one, copying the prey's movement, like the hopping of the springhaas. The signal for vervet monkey (*opposite page, 3rd row, right*) mimics neither movement nor appearance; it is simply an upturned palm indicating that the vervet is "like a man." (Howell, *Early Man*, 184–85)

Photographs by Irven DeVore, courtesy of Anthro-Photo.

SPRINGHAAS

BAT-EARED FOX

PANGOLIN

GREATER KUDU

GIRAFFE

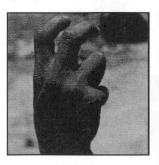

HARTEBEEST

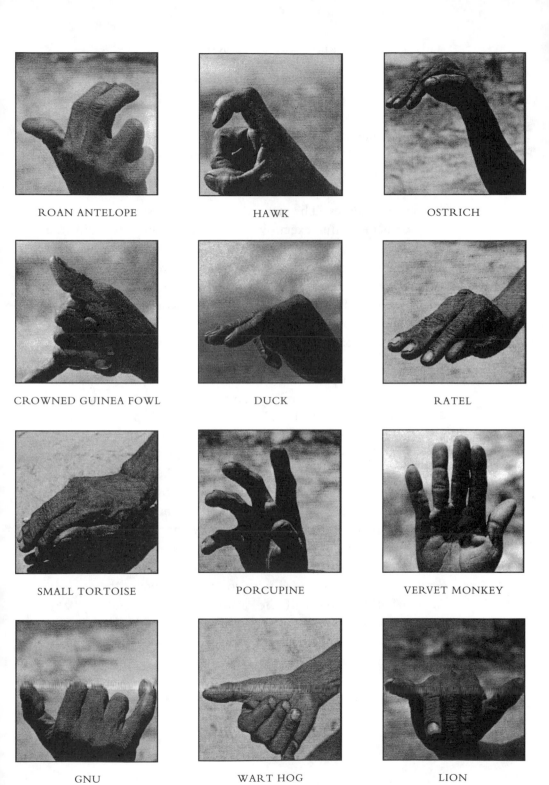

ROAN ANTELOPE

HAWK

OSTRICH

CROWNED GUINEA FOWL

DUCK

RATEL

SMALL TORTOISE

PORCUPINE

VERVET MONKEY

GNU

WART HOG

LION

would be seen as the seat of attention and volition, but not as an idealized language organ grinding out abstract syntactic rules. The proposed cortical areas seem very much grounded in the management of complex movements in the case of the supplementary motor area, and in crossmodal association of sensory input in the case of the inferior parietal lobe. In this recasting of the homunculus, its role would remain grounded in the real world of human actions and senses. The natural selective pressures behind the development of this executive system may have been directed more at the growing cognitive power needed to handle and sequence complex and simultaneous multimodal behavioral streams, rather than that needed to generate abstract, hierarchical data structures. Donald argues that such a working memory system could not possibly have the power to carry out the sorts of linguistic and cognitive tasks that literate, modern humans engage in—an external symbolic storage system is needed for that.

In addition to providing a clue as to how the brain may have acquired its power to construct complex sentences, a view of the interrelatedness of speech and sign may also provide some insight into the transition from iconic signs to symbolic spoken words. If, as has already been suggested, iconic visible signs are plausible candidates for the first genuine hominid words, then habitual pairings of signs with vocal utterances provides an almost perversely simple mechanism for introducing more abstract and symbolic spoken words. A model for this is suggested by the iconic handshapes, designating prey, of the !Kung hunters of the Kalahari.[35] At an early stage of language, such iconic or mimetic signs for animals could have been combined with sounds imitative of the animals' calls or other aspects of the animals' behavior (see fig. 22). Eventually these sounds, after modification, could stand alone as symbols that no longer resembled the sounds made by the animals in an iconic way. Call this the "sign-chatter" hypothesis, an idea that goes back at least as far as Condillac. We have already seen that early hominids were probably quite voluble, as are chimpanzees. Over the course of millennia, other patterns of sound could become habitually associated with specific visible signs. Such associations continue today in the ordinary communicative behavior of hearing speakers and comprise the norm for most human communication. One can argue, moreover, that this simple observation about the simultaneous association of word and visible sign can be applied to one of the most intractable problems in Western philosophy and psychology—the problem of meaning.

Notes

1. Le Gros Clark (1963, 228).
2. Mirzoeff (1995, 190).
3. For a recent summary of this information, see Deacon (1997, 228–309).
4. van Marle (1994, 2927–30), and see Jakobson (1956).
5. Eisenson (1962, 52).
6. Newcombe et al. (1965).
7. Bogen (1973, 107f).
8. Dimond (1972, 176).
9. See Armstrong (1987).
10. Brownell et al. (1983); Wapner, Hamby, and Gardner (1981); Winner and Gardner (1977).
11. Edwards (1989).
12. Kimura (1993).
13. Gannon et al. (1998).
14. Stokoe (1960, 45).
15. Hockett (1978, 274).
16. Kimura (1981).
17. Poizner and Lane (1979).
18. Söderfeldt, Rönnberg, and Risberg (1994).
19. Kimura (1993).
20. Kimura (1976).
21. Bonvillian and Richards (1993).
22. Wilcox (1996).
23. McNeill (1992); Kendon (1997); and Farnell (1995).
24. Peters (1990).
25. Johnson, Liddell, and Erting (1989) call SimCom "Sign Supported Speech."
26. Messing (1994).
27. Farnell (1995).

28. Groce (1985).

29. In his paper on the Yucatec Maya, Robert E. Johnson (1991), an anthropological linguist at Gallaudet University, also mentions unpublished reports of similar situations in Venezuela, Africa, and on the Navaho reservation in Arizona.

30. Branson, Miller, and Masaja (1996).

31. Groce (1985, 60).

32. Johnson, Liddell, and Erting (1989).

33. Padden (1990).

34. Donald (1991, 326–31).

35. Howell (1965). See Uniker-Sebeok and Sebeok (1978) and Kendon (1989) for descriptions of aboriginal sign systems in the Americas and Australia.

6 | The Morning Star and the Evening Star

WE HAVE LEFT the most difficult question for last. How do we know what words and sentences mean? To answer this question, we must first ask what it means to mean something. Here it is necessary to distinguish between the concepts of meaning and reference. Philosophers have long understood that the meaning of an utterance is not the same as the thing to which it refers. The most famous example illustrating the distinction between meaning and reference is probably that put forward by Gottlob Frege, a German philosopher of the late nineteenth and early twentieth centuries, who pointed out that the terms *morning star* and *evening star* referred to the same celestial body (generally the planet Venus) but had quite different meanings. As Quine points out, the fact that only one celestial body was involved was probably first established by a Babylonian astronomer, "[b]ut the two phrases cannot be regarded as having the same meaning; otherwise that Babylonian could have dispensed with his observations and contented himself with reflecting on the meanings of his words."[1]

Several pairs of terms have been applied to this essential difference: *meaning* (or *sense*) and *reference* (or *naming*), *intension* and *extension,* and *connotation* and *denotation*. In general, and quite simplistically, the extension of a term is the range of objects to which it refers or which it denotes. The intension of a term is the set of attributes that it connotes or the set of rules in the language for its proper use. In this respect, the term *connotation* has a different sense from its use in ordinary language, where it is generally understood to refer to the associations that accrue to a term as it is used in a particular language. So, the extension of the terms *morning star* and *evening star* is the same—they refer to the same physical object, but their intensions are different—different attributes (appearance in the evening vs. appearance in the morning) are connoted. Some readers may suspect that what is being revealed here is the irrelevant tip of a trivial iceberg of philosophical disputation. Others may suspect that an obscure sort of confidence game is afoot, and it is certainly not the purpose of this chapter to attempt to present or analyze the many obscure yet heated debates that philosophers have carried on concerning the significance of these terms. However, for the rest of the discussion to make sense, the reader must have at least a superficial understanding of how these terms have been used.

Perhaps the easiest way to think about this is to put ourselves in the place of a linguist who is trying to decipher a language that he has never heard before. The philosopher Willard Van Orman Quine puts the usual solution to the problem and the further problems that it raises trenchantly: "The nature of this entering wedge into a strange lexicon encourages the misconception of meaning as reference, since words at this stage are construed, typically, by pointing to the object referred to."[2] This point, of course, was also recognized long ago by Amos Kendall in the quotation that was given at the beginning of this book. We take pointing to be perhaps the most elementary of signifying activities, and this simple act figures in numerous branches of knowledge—semiotics and philosophy for example—under a variety of terms such as *index, deixis,* and *ostension.* It is, perhaps, inevitable to think of pointing evolving as a signifying act out of the equally fundamental act of reaching out and grasping an object.

Quine, however, wants us to think about something much more complex than the simple act of pointing—he asks how we can know exactly what the speaker of a language that is unknown to us means when he points at an object. He gives the following famous example—a linguist doing research on a previously unknown population hears one of the "natives" utter the word *gavagai* while simultaneously pointing at a rabbit. Does the native mean what we mean when we say the word *rabbit?*

> Who knows but what the objects to which this term applies are not rabbits after all, but mere stages, or brief temporal segments, of rabbits? . . . Or perhaps the objects to which 'gavagai' applies are all and sundry undetached parts of rabbits. . . . Nothing not distinguished in stimulus meaning itself is to be distinguished by pointing, unless the pointing is accompanied by questions of identity and diversity "Is this the same gavagai as that?" "Do we have here one gavagai or two?"[3]

Here Quine states the fundamental problem recognized by Whorf and Sapir: How can we know how people foreign from us segment and order the world? Perhaps even more difficult is the question posed in a book by the psychologist David Premack bearing the title *Gavagai:* How can we know what an animal of another species, in this case a chimpanzee, means when it communicates with us?[4] It should come as no surprise that the position taken here is that understanding the evolutionary history of the two species can help us in this regard.

We can put this problem into more concrete and familiar terms by thinking about what we mean when we say the English word *chair.* Think of this in terms of the notion of extension given above: the range of objects to which the word *chair* refers. When we hear the word *chair,* most of us will have no difficulty visualizing things with four legs, a seat, and a back on which one person can sit. But is it still a chair if more than one person can sit on it? Or if it doesn't have a back? Or if it is the place where the king usually sits? The idea of fuzzy logic might help us here—perhaps we should think in terms of prototypical chairs gradually merging into categories that are less chairlike. These issues become important when we move beyond a view of grammar that implies operations as simple as selecting words according to part of speech and inserting them into slots or the nodes of a logical tree. Fairly complicated judgments are involved in deciding whether something is a chair, a bench, a stool, or a throne. This observation also points to the idea that words have complex semantic interrelationships that interact in complex ways with their possible syntactic relationships in sentences. In some contexts, one or another of the possible terms to denote an object may be more appropriate than in some other contexts. For example, consider this sentence: "A throne is a chair that a monarch sits on during ceremonial occasions."

In his book, *The Symbolic Species,* Terrence Deacon approaches this problem from a somewhat different perspective, employing the terminology and semiotic theory of Charles Sanders Peirce. Deacon suggests, based on studies of the linguistic abilities of chimpanzees by Sue Savage-Rumbaugh and Duane Rumbaugh, that what is involved is not so much learning what is included in the domain of a sign as what is excluded. For a symbolic system to work effectively as a communication system, it must segment the world fairly completely—large chunks of the possible universe of discourse cannot go unaccounted for, and it is our ability to acquire such a comprehensive symbolic *system* that Deacon believes separates us from apes, at least in terms of having exploited much more fully an underlying pre-adaptation. In particular, it appears that chimpanzees must be taught the functional domains of symbols, something that human beings seem to accomplish through induction, without specific training. Return for a moment to the example of the word *chair.* A normal child who is acquiring English has little difficulty sorting out and learning to use appropriately the categories chair, bench, stool, and throne, and the child has little difficulty understanding that the categories of things referred to are related and can be overlapping. According to this argument, chimpanzees learn with relative ease to associate signs for objects with individual objects in an indexical manner, but they have much more difficulty and need much more training to develop the ability to use appropriately in combination symbols that refer to such interrelated categories. But even here, as Deacon notes, the extraordinary abilities of Savage-Rumbaugh's bonobo Kanzi may belie attempts to specify rigid species differences.[5]

Before we proceed with more detailed treatment of what this possible species difference implies, some discussion of Peirce's unique place in American intellectual history is in order. Peirce was an American original whose writings ranged over natural history, mathematics, and philosophy, but perhaps partly because of his failure to obtain a regular academic position his work was relatively unknown during a career that spanned the last third of the nineteenth century and the first decade of the twentieth. He is now well known for his contributions to the philosophical school known as pragmatism and to semiotics, but as a compiler of his most significant writings remarks pointedly: "Among thinkers of the first rank, few have in their lifetime addressed so small a public as Peirce."[6]

Deacon introduces one of Peirce's interlocking classifications of signs, that which classifies them as *icons, indices,* or *symbols.*[7] We have encountered these terms throughout this book, but they have been used somewhat loosely. To understand Deacon's argument, we will have to define these terms roughly as Peirce did in his theory of signs, or *semiotics.* Each sign presupposes a triad, described as follows:

> A sign, or *representamen,* is something which stands to somebody for something in some respect or capacity. It addresses somebody, that is, creates in the mind of that person an equivalent sign, or perhaps a more developed sign. That sign which it creates I call the *interpretant* of the first sign. The sign stands for something, its *object.* It stands for that object, not in all respects, but in reference to a sort of idea, which I have sometimes called the *ground* of the representamen.[8]

This triad consists then of an object to be represented, what we might call a sign *vehicle* to represent it, and someone to interpret the representation. The types of signs—icons, indices, and symbols—are to be understood with respect to this triad of relationships.

According to Peirce, an icon is a sign by virtue of being like its object in some way. Icons include pictures, diagrams, and so on.

An index is a sign by virtue of having a direct physical relationship with its object. The most obvious type of index involves, simply, pointing. Symbols involve conventional or lawful relationships, and would include the ordinary words of a language. Peirce also defines these terms with respect to their relationships with their objects and interpretants:

> An *icon* is a sign which would lose the character which renders it significant even though its object had no existence; such as a lead-pencil streak as representing a geometrical line. An *index* is a sign which would, at once, lose the character which makes it a sign if its object were removed, but would not lose that character if there were no interpretant. Such, for instance, is a piece of mould with a bullet-hole in it as sign of a shot; for without the shot there would have been no hole; but there is a hole there, whether any-body has the sense to attribute it to a shot or not. A *symbol* is a sign which would lose the character which renders it a sign if there were no interpretant. Such is any utterance of speech which signi-fies what it does only by virtue of its being understood to have that signification.[9]

To this point, Peirce's theory would seem to be addressing pri-marily the question of how reference is established. But further consideration of it leads deeper into questions of meaning and the interrelationships among signs and among types of signs, and no precise delineation is in fact possible among these types of signs. A single sign may have aspects of more than one type. According to Peirce: "Symbols grow. They come into being by development out of other signs, particularly from icons, or from mixed signs partaking of the nature of icons and symbols."[10] The unique opportunity that study of signed languages affords us, if we can put aside our biases both old and new, is that of seeing this growth process proceeding literally before our eyes. We can see what were originally icons becoming full-fledged symbols, we can see pantomime being compressed into a more confined "phonologi-cal" space with many of the characteristics of speech. And we can begin to imagine how symbolic speech must have emerged from mimesis in both the visual-gestural and vocal-gestural modes.

In 1800 the poet Samuel Taylor Coleridge wrote the following in a letter to a friend: "Is *Thinking* impossible without arbitrary signs? And how far is the word "arbitrary" a misnomer? Are not words, etc., parts and germinations of the plant? And what is the law of their growth? In something of this sort I would endeavour to destroy the old antithesis of Words and Things; elevating, as it were, Words into Things and living things too."[11] The laws of growth of symbols may involve the establishment of a hierarchy of icons, indices, and symbols, as Deacon suggests, but symbols also grow by accretion, by association with other signs. If we see words and sentences emerging first through mimetic gesture, we can begin to discern a process whereby meaningful "arbitrary" signs and words could emerge through a natural, "organic" progression from icons and indices to fully arbitrary symbols.

Deacon correctly recognizes that these terms, when applied to the signs of a signed language, are not absolute:

> [T]here was at one time considerable debate over whether hand signs in American Sign Language (ASL) are iconic or symbolic. Many signs seemed to resemble pantomime or appeared graphically to "depict" or point to what was represented, and so some researchers suggested that their meaning was "merely iconic" and by implication, not wordlike. It is now abundantly clear, however, that despite such resemblances, ASL is a language and its elements are both symbolic and wordlike in every regard. Being capable of iconic or indexical interpretation in no way diminishes these signs' capacity of being interpreted symbolically as well. These modes of reference aren't mutually exclusive alternatives; though at any one time only one of these modes may be prominent, the same signs can be icons, indices, or symbols depending on the interpretive process.[12]

However, it will not do to imply what Deacon implies here— that these iconic and indexic items are simply "recruited" into ASL and "recoded" linguistically to act like entirely arbitrary words. As Scott Liddell has shown with respect to pointing in ASL, it is simply impossible to understand how the language works, why it is organized the way it is, without recognizing its fundamental connection to indexicality.[13] Moreover, as we have seen and will see, recognizing these as formative processes in signed languages can help us to see how meaning develops in language in general.

Gilbert Eastman, a deaf scholar and actor, demonstrates this process at work in an ASL instructional manual entitled *From Mime to Sign*. Eastman shows clearly how complex ASL utterances can be built up from iconic and mimetic "classifiers" designating shape, number, and so on. He also shows how facial and other bodily gestures are incorporated into ASL, and, perhaps most important, he insists on the continuity between the basic gestures of ASL and those employed by ordinary hearing speakers of American English. In fact, he uses this continuity as an "entering wedge," *à la* Quine, into ASL for hearing speakers of English.[14] As Eastman and many other deaf people have always understood, at least implicitly, we do not denigrate or devalue the signed languages of deaf people by recognizing their fundamental grounding in visible gesture. What we *should* do is avoid setting up false dichotomies between "words" and "gestures" and recognize these signed languages as expressions of the common inheritance of all human beings. If we are able to keep our minds open and if we accept the arguments presented in this book, we might also recognize that it is at least partly through the use of such communication systems that we became *fully* human beings and that the human community would be diminished if we no longer had them (see fig. 23).

Let us return then to a question that we posed earlier—how can we know what other people mean? For that matter, how can we know what other people think, or even perceive? This is the age-old problem of solipsism, and we certainly do not want to approach that philosophical black hole. Chomsky offers a simple answer. We know what other people mean because their brains, or the parts of their brains that use language, are constructed like ours, so they segment the world in much the same way that we do. Their words fall into roughly the same categories as ours. We

"Columns seen from a distance"

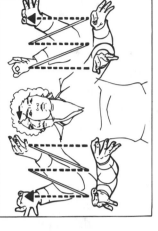

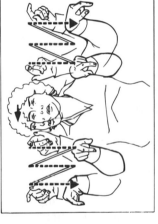

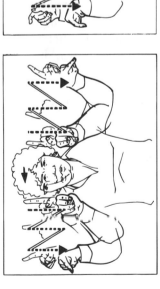

1 handshape
"parallel lines"

G handshape
"parallel lines with some width"

F handshape
"narrow parallel columns"

"Columns seen from close-up"

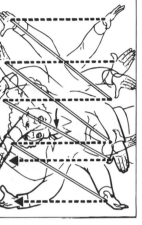

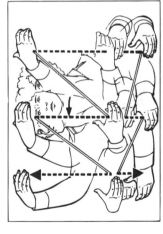

C handshape
"huge parallel columns"

C handshape
"large parallel columns"

Fig. 23. A signer describing the columns of the U.S. Capitol as seen from varying distances. Reprinted, by permission of the publisher, from *American Sign Language: A Teacher's Resource Text on Grammar and Culture* by Charlotte Baker-Shenk and Dennis Cokely (Washington, D.C.: Gallaudet University Press, 1991), 320.

can now see another possibility—that their *actions* in the world are like ours in some fundamental ways, and the act of signifying grows out of more basic practical actions. This approach to the problem permits us to see a universal grounding for language, while at the same time allowing for the variation that anthropological and sign linguists have revealed. Recall our earlier discussion of semantic phonology, where some of the movements and forms of individual signs were said to have some of the attributes of nouns and verbs, the most basic categories of generative grammars. But recall also that these aspects of signs are present simultaneously and thus cannot be said to be categorical in the manner that is implied by the grammatical categories noun and verb.

We can apply this observation to an old debate that was presumed to have been settled by the Chomskyan revolution but that continues to resurface. Is it true that categories such as noun and verb can necessarily always be applied productively to some non-Indo-European languages? Here we need to revisit a passage from Whorf describing the Hopi language that was quoted in chapter 2:

> They are not set up as entities that can function in a sentence like terms for people, animals, or masses of matter having characteristic form, or again, human groups and human relations, but are treated as PURELY RELATIONAL CONCEPTS, of an adverbial type. Thus hollow spaces like room, chamber, hall, are not really NAMED as objects are, but are rather LOCATED, i.e., positions of other things are specified so as to show their location in such hollow spaces.[15]

Can we simply assume that the grammatical processes at work in languages like Hopi or ASL are completely described by the standard grammatical categories that have been used traditionally to describe Indo-European languages and that are now used in generative grammar theory? It used to be believed that ASL did not have *true* verbs and nouns, but processes used by signers to distinguish these categories have since been described. These processes were first noted by Ted Supalla and Elissa Newport,[16] deaf and hearing collaborators. However, when we look at ASL from the perspective of semantic phonology, we can see that this issue, with respect to the dynamic presentation of actual utterances, may, in fact, be quite complex—the categories themselves may be in dynamic flux. Whorf called attention to similar difficulties with respect to spoken languages that are radically different from English.

Some of the vivid examples of what might be called Whorfisms are surely wrong, at least some of the things that have been attributed to Whorf in the lore of modern linguistics (but that he may never have said). The most widely cited example concerns the number of words that Eskimos have for snow, said by some to be as many as one hundred or more. Suffice it say that no Eskimo language (depending on how one defines "word") has anything like this number of words for snow (English, of course, also has many words for snow—slush, sleet, etc.), but also suffice it to say that Whorf himself never made this claim.[17] What Whorf, and Franz Boas before him,[18] were claiming was that Eskimo languages apparently had no "blanket" term for snow in general. Their claim was that Eskimo languages require the speaker to say something more than just "snow," such as "snow on the ground" or "falling snow." But Dell Hymes is also surely right that "languages differ in their makeup as adaptive resources."[19] Although language and thought are not the same thing, if you have words for more things, you can talk about more things, and you can think about more things. The problem that Whorf, Sapir, and Quine have identified is that to understand a language you must understand, at some level, the culture of the people who speak it. You must understand what has been called their Weltanschauung or worldview. This has been put in somewhat different terms by Wittgenstein: "To imagine a language means to imagine a form of life."[20]

To get a sense of how pervasive this problem is in human affairs, consider an issue that arises perennially in American politics, and is generally put in terms of loose versus strict construction of the U.S. Constitution. Arguments arise periodically over just what the Founding Fathers meant by certain clauses in the

Constitution. When they wrote a clause guaranteeing citizens the right to keep and bear arms in the Second Amendment but appended it to another clause about the need for maintaining well-ordered militias, were they guaranteeing the right absolutely or only within limited contexts? To support their arguments, constitutional scholars periodically attempt to get inside the heads of the drafters. What might they have meant by "militia," for example? Because we are now separated from them by some two hundred years, and because ways of life and the words used to describe them change in form and meaning, how should we interpret certain of the document's passages? Is it even important any longer to attempt to divine their "exact" meanings? As we saw in chapter 4, it is arguable whether such a document could survive as long as this one has if its meaning were always perfectly clear. But multiply this problem by fifty when our task is to get inside the heads of New Guinea highlanders living as our ancestors lived ten thousand years ago.

How do we get from simple pointing to the construction of a world? Does it require a macromutation rearranging the structures of the brains of our hominid ancestors? After our discussion of the emergence of meaning, we can see clearly why this argument is unnecessary. What is crucial is understanding that there are underlying relationships among words and signs that go beyond the construction of the logical relationships that are specified by syntax. This is what is implied by the idea of connotation in its ordinary language sense. Consider the sort of obligatory grammatical categories, such as shape and gender, that some languages employ and that were introduced in chapter 2. The effect of these semantic markers is to establish large association sets among units that receive the same marker. Stretching the sense of connotation somewhat to include what Whorf has called "these thousands of linkage processes,"[21] one can suggest that the effect of these semantic markers is to extend the connotation of the words that receive them. Again, gender in Indo-European nouns is a familiar example. Assignment of a noun to a gender class (male, female, neuter) is *nonreferential;* that is, such assignment does not ordinarily lead to a distinction among objects, because reference is already accomplished by the noun (NAME) itself. However, in languages in which nouns have gender, such assignment may be essential to its *meaning.* We can see how these "connotational" connections might arise first out of physical resemblances among signs, based on their iconic resemblances to physically similar objects. These linkages would then naturally be carried over into more symbolic and arbitrary spoken communication. In the final analysis, this richness of association is what gives languages their symbolic power.

When we take into account these sorts of underlying, nonsyntactic relationships among the words and signs of languages, it becomes possible to see why another tenet of modern linguistics breaks down under some conditions. Under the Chomskyan paradigm, everything in one language should be more or less perfectly translatable into any other language. But some things are simply not. Take Lévi-Strauss's title, *La Pensée Sauvage,* usually translated into English as *The Savage Mind.* First, the word *sauvage* in French means "wild" or "uncivilized" and does not appear to have as strongly negative connotations as the cognate English word *savage* so a better translation might be *The Uncivilized Mind,* which, of course, has much less panache than the original. But as the dust jacket of the French edition makes clear, the title is also a pun—meaning in French "the wild pansy" (the dust jacket bears a picture of this flower). This pun cannot be translated into English adequately unless one adds extensive notes, such as those contained in this paragraph. In this respect the problem of translation is not different from the problem of definition (that is, explaining the meaning of a word), which usually proceeds, in Quine's terms, by the invocation of "lame synonyms plus stage directions."[22] Many English-speaking anthropologists would not be surprised to learn that Lévi-Strauss chose his title at least partly to frustrate attempts at translation.

Wordplay and so-called "figurative" language in general pose problems for translators. As metaphors go, this familiar one from Alfred Noyes's *The Highwayman* certainly ranks high on the vividness scale:

The moon was a ghostly galleon tossed upon cloudy seas.

This sentence is not meaningful in the terms of traditional linguistics—the moon is not a ship, and this metaphor would be difficult to translate into many other languages. People who have reached a certain level of sophistication in the English language will recognize this sentence as counterfactual but nevertheless meaningful. It clearly is not intended to convey information about the moon, but rather to evoke a mental image. Of course, much has been written and said about the function of metaphor and other figurative language beyond this simple observation about mental imagery. What is most important to this discussion is that metaphors are classified by Peirce as *icons*. Here is an example of the apparent hierarchical structure among the linguistic signs of a language. What is clearly symbolic at one level—for example, the word *galleon*—is part of an icon (the metaphor itself) at another. Icons are here interpreted as mental images, which for human beings generally mean visual images. What is proposed, then, is that metaphor provides a fundamental bridge between our primary sensory system—vision—and the sensory medium through which most of us express language—audition. One of the functions of metaphor, then, is to "visualize" languages that are expressed in terms of auditory symbols, providing otherwise arbitrary signs an anchor in the "iconic" visible world.

Just as the moon is not a ship, it is not made of green cheese either, although some people may at some time have believed that to be true. Such a statement about the moon is clearly meaningful, and it might be classified as simply a statement of belief that, following the success of NASA's Apollo program, has been shown to be false. Many other well-known expressions, while true, are meaningless in that they do not convey new information—for example, the following used to be seen on bumper stickers in the United States: "When guns are outlawed, only outlaws will have guns." This statement is, of course, tautological—any English noun can be substituted for "guns" and the expression will continue to be true (e.g., "When bidets are outlawed, only outlaws will have bidets"). The meaning of the original expression lies not in its referential power, or in its power as a proposition, but in its emblematic function of identifying the driver of the car as a right-thinking defender of the Second Amendment of the U.S. Constitution. Of course to others it identifies the driver as a right-wing, reactionary Neandertal.

Many other words refer to nonexistent entities—unicorns, dragons, and so on—but have meaning. Can they be said to refer to anything? In some philosophical considerations, they might be said to refer to "unactualized possibles," or ideas in the mind.[23] We can imagine, and even draw a picture of, a horse with a single horn growing from its nose or a giant, flying, fire-breathing reptile. If we have encountered sleepwalkers or have spouses who toss and turn at night, we can even imagine "furious sleep." We could also, at least metaphorically, imagine ideas becoming dormant, going to sleep as it were, only to be "reawakened" through acts of rediscovery. But how about "colorless green ideas"—these are "logical impossibilities," aren't they? Not only do they not refer to anything, but the phrase describing them must also be meaningless, right? Of course, we can insert the phrase "colorless green ideas" into what everyone would agree is a meaningful sentence; for example, "There are no such things as colorless green ideas," but Chomsky has challenged us to deal with the whole sentence including that phrase. Nevertheless, some of us may have the nagging feeling that this particular sentence now has such currency, at least among people who read books like this one, that it has somehow acquired a certain measure of meaningfulness, as in these lines from the poem "Coiled Alizarine," dedicated to Noam Chomsky by John Hollander.

> Curiously deep, the slumber of crimson thoughts:
> While breathless, in stodgy viridian,
> Colorless green ideas sleep furiously.[24]

So the sentence works somehow. It works because it (or parts of it) has become a token for something else, it has become a sign at another level—perhaps a metaphor for the mental labors of those who think about these arcane ideas.

Many of the questions that we have explored so far remain unanswered and much of our subject is shrouded in mystery. We can only hope that much of it will remain so. The last words on this subject are left to Baudelaire, and they are the words with which we began this book:

> In Nature's temple living pillars rise,
> And words are murmured that none have understood,
> And man must wander through forests of symbols,
> That watch him with familiar eyes.[25]

Notes

1. Quine (1953, 9).
2. Ibid. (62).
3. Quine (1960, 51–53).
4. Premack (1986).
5. Deacon (1997, 69–101).
6. Buchler (1955, ix).
7. Deacon (1997, 69–101).
8. Buchler (1955, 99).
9. Ibid. (104).
10. Ibid. (115).
11. See Shattuck (1985, 201).
12. Deacon (1997, 72).
13. Liddell (1996).
14. Eastman (1989).
15. Whorf (1956, 202).
16. Supalla and Newport (1978).

17. In fact, Whorf (1956, 216) refers to five different types of snow that Eskimos might refer to with different terms.

18. Boas ([1911] 1963, 191), who had done fieldwork with Eskimos in Canada, mentions four separate terms.

19. Hymes (1973, 78f).

20. Schulte (1992, 108).

21. Whorf (1956, 68).

22. Quine (1953, 58). See Leach (1970, 87–88).

23. Ibid. (5).

24. Hollander (1974).

25. From "*Correspondances,*" by Charles Baudelaire. Translation from the French by the author, after a translation in Huneker (1919, 24).

7 | Forked Tongues

IF SPOKEN LANGUAGE arose in a manner similar to that proposed in this book, a question of perennial interest remains—how and why did languages, both spoken and signed, become so diverse? Why would peoples, living side by side over generations, maintain separate languages, vastly different in terms of pronunciation, lexicon, and grammar, thereby impeding commerce, promoting enmity, and perhaps even warfare, among neighboring peoples? The Bible gives us an explanation in the story of the Tower of Babel.[1] Human beings committed the sin of arrogance by attempting to build a tower up to the heavens, so God punished them by giving them different languages, thus dividing them and making it impossible for them to cooperate again on such a grand scale. Perhaps a better explanation for the diversification of language comes from another biblical account, this one of the Gileadites identifying their defeated and fleeing enemies by forcing them to pronounce the word "shibboleth." The Hebrew dialect of the Ephraimites did not include the "sh" sound, so they pronounced the word "sibboleth" and were executed. The Book of Judges records that forty-two thousand were thus slain.[2]

If we hypothesize that there is an upper limit on the size of social groups that can be organized effectively simply through mechanisms of face-to-face interaction, it becomes possible to understand why it is so useful for human beings to be able to distinguish absolutely and easily between in-group and out-group members. In this regard, differences in language between groups could serve the function, as Hymes terms it, of "boundary maintenance" between groups. Boundary maintenance devices could work at the level of entirely separate language groups as well as to identify class differences within groups. When Professor Higgins asks "Why can't the English learn to speak?"[3] he is really reflecting on a rigidly enforced boundary maintenance device separating the recognized classes within English society. What used to be called "Black English" and which now goes, at least in some circles, by the name "Ebonics" serves a similar function in American society, although it is also associated with differences in physical appearance. Sherman Wilcox has identified a similar mechanism at work in the signing of a group of deaf students in an educational program in New Mexico.[4] Wilcox studied the deaf students' use of a particular sign, generally glossed in English as "STUCK." Its usage in ASL suggests that its range of meaning is much like that of the English word *stuck,* as in "your truck is stuck in the mud," or "I am stuck in the elevator." The sign is made by moving the V, or "Victory," hand toward the signer's neck, as though to skewer it. Wilcox found an interesting semantic extension of the sign, among this particular group of students, to something like the American English expression "gotcha." The students appeared to be using the sign to ridicule their hearing teachers, who apparently remained ignorant of its use in this manner. James Woodward and Harry Markowicz, ASL linguists working at Gallaudet University, have noted that the use by deaf people of a vernacular ASL which is relatively inaccessible to hearing people can be seen as a boundary maintenance device, while systems like SimCom may function as a buffer between the deaf and hearing communities, allowing the maintenance of the more inaccessible vernacular.[5] All of these devices seem to have the function of delineating the boundaries of separately operating social groups, and the nonstandard languages that define socially subordinate groups are often viewed with ambivalence by those who use them. Although these languages are symbols of group solidarity, they may also be instruments of oppression.

These processes of delineation and diversification may have operated originally from one wellspring or from many. Whether the languages that we see today had one source or many has been a hotly contested question that has no sensible answer, and no attempt will be made to provide one here. But it is necessary to ask again why hominids exploited the possibilities of symbolic communication during the last five million years when chimpanzees did not. The most plausible current explanation was outlined in chapter 1 in terms of the presumed exploitation by the hominids of a new environment. Success in this endeavor appears to have been based upon the introduction of a new social structure involving increased division of labor and, consequently, the need for enhanced communication about events occurring at remote locations and for the storage of symbolically encoded information about the environment.

Is it possible at this point to speculate about when major milestones were reached in the evolution of the capacity for this sort of communication? This has certainly been attempted. Many attempts at specifying the beginning point for language "as we know it" have focused on the Upper Paleolithic (the last part of the Old Stone Age), the point at which representational "art" begins to appear, roughly forty thousand years ago.[6] When this is claimed to be the most likely starting point for fully modern, fully recursive language, the argument usually put forward is that the appearance of representational art, best known in the remarkable cave paintings of France and Spain, is the first sure sign we have of human symbolic abilities (see fig. 24). However, this is a very late point on the evolutionary path, originating five million years ago, that led to modern human beings. According to this argument human beings would have been using fully their most important behavioral system for perhaps less than 1% of their separate evolutionary history. Other proposals for the time of onset of fully articulate speech would set this event at the time of the appearance of fully modern *Homo sapiens,* probably between one hundred thousand and two hundred thousand years ago. This argument usually revolves around the evidence for lack of a fully modern vocal tract before this time. Working against this argument is the observation that a brain as large as that of modern human beings has been around for at least four hundred thousand years amongst what is usually called archaic *Homo sapiens*. It is important here to reiterate what was said in the first chapter—there can be no definitive answer to the question. However, it does seem fair to speculate that at least as far back as the time of *Homo erectus*, human beings

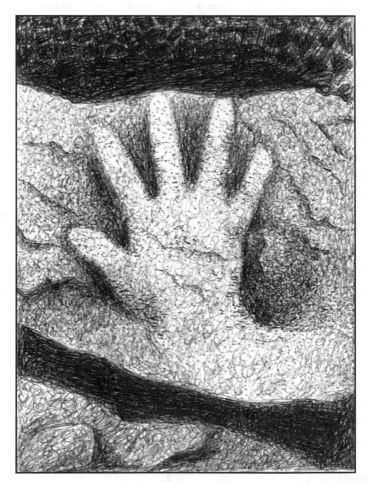

Fig. 24. Impression of a human hand from El Castillo cave, Santander, Spain. Redrawn by Robert C. Johnson after a photograph in Jacob Bronowski, *The Ascent of Man* (Boston: Little, Brown, 1973).

would have had the anatomical and neurological capability to engage in fairly sophisticated forms of communication involving both signing and speech. Whether or not one wants to speculate that this might have been *language* may depend ultimately on how one defines the term.

After language first developed, what paths did its diversification follow? As was suggested above, Western traditions about how languages came to be so diverse can be traced to the biblical story of the Tower of Babel. The Book of Genesis also contains an explanation for the diversification of human biological populations—they are all derived from the three sons of Noah: Shem, Ham, and Japheth. But this story also contains the seeds of an association between race and language that has been endemic to Western thought and that anthropology spent much of its time in the twentieth century trying to disprove. The names Shem and Ham are current in linguistic classifications today, in the names for the dominant language families of the Middle East (Semitic) and North Africa (Hamitic), respectively. We can even find a Cushitic group of languages in Africa after Cush, one of the sons of Ham, and in some traditional accounts, Indo-European populations are said to be descended from Japheth. This biblical story has even been used to justify racism and African slavery, Noah having cursed the descendants of Ham and assigned to them the role of servants or slaves. In the biblical tradition, then, human languages and races derive, literally, from a "family tree."[7]

Now, the usual way of representing linguistic diversity from a historical point of view is to represent the groups of languages known to have historical relationships in terms of a tree diagram. With respect to the diversification of languages, the version of these diagrams most familiar to readers of this book would be one representing Indo-European languages. Proto-Indo-European would form the trunk of the tree, with the various subfamilies of Indo-European branching downward from the trunk. Such tree diagrams have also been used to describe the diversification of the human populations with respect to racial affinity. However, dichotomous tree diagrams may not be the most appropriate models for describing either the genetic or the linguistic histories of large proportions of the world's current and former populations.

When we are dealing with biological populations, branching tree diagrams are most appropriate to the description of populations that are known to be diverging or that have diverged genetically, that is, at the species level and above. Separate species are defined as populations that do not or can not interbreed. It is arguable whether they may also be usefully applied at the subspecific or racial level to populations that experience extremely limited gene flow over long periods of time. Human beings are the most adaptable of the mammals, and it is unlikely that any pair of modern human populations is or was headed toward intergroup infertility or speciation. This is well illustrated in the history of the peopling of the American continents, where tree diagrams would be of little help in sorting out the genetic relationships among the current populations. The underlying problem can be seen in the convoluted definitions that are used by U.S. governmental agencies in the pursuit of illusory racial identifications of modern Americans. This is not to say that race is not important in modern America—it is indeed important, but as a social, not a biological concept. For example, the traditional definition of "black" or "African" American applies to anyone whose appearance suggests any trace of African ancestry, even if the majority of an individual's ancestors can be traced to Europe or Asia. Thus we have the curious contemporary case of the golfer Tiger Woods, usually said to be an "African American," even though only about one quarter of his known ancestors actually originated from Africa. The use of tree diagrams to describe human subspecific or racial variation has thus had a controversial history, and because of the reasons just given and the abuses of racism, they are seldom used for this purpose in physical anthropology today.

Similar trends are found in studies of linguistic diversity, but tree diagrams abound. The question is not whether trees *can* be used to represent the underlying relationships, but whether they represent the *most appropriate* models, given the possibility that anastomoses, or rejoinings, of linguistic stocks (and subspecific biological populations) may so readily occur. The origin of English provides a familiar example of the problem. It is common to place modern English at the end of a branch of the Germanic group of Indo-European languages, because of the known history of its speakers and elements of its core vocabulary and sound system. One could argue, however, on the basis of lexical and syntactic features, that it is really Italic and not Germanic, closely related to modern French. The truth, of course, is that it is neither—it is descended from an amalgam of Anglo-Saxon and Norman French and has evolved subsequently for a millennium relatively independently of other Germanic languages. The tendency to place modern English and French at the ends of two ramified branches having a common ancestor as remote as Proto-Indo-European grossly distorts the actual relationship between the two languages and their speakers (see fig. 25), and the situation of English may be more typical than unique in human history.[8]

A Platonic view of language encourages us to see these trees as representing irreversible bifurcations. This applies to sign and speech, as well as to historically related spoken languages. Instead of downward branching trees as representations of the historical relationships among languages, imagine instead a reticular, or net-like structure stretched over a sphere (globe) and growing steadily outward through time. And as a representation of the relationships among the words or signs of any *particular* language, imagine Darwin's "tangled bank" of complexly intertwined and interdependent organisms. The diagram from an early classic of physical anthropology, E. A. Hooton's 1932 book *Up from the Ape,*[9] represents an attempt to deal with some of the problems created by the use of tree diagrams to represent human subspecific biological variation (see fig. 26). Note that virtually all of the "racial" terms used to describe this variation are now considered "politically incorrect." No current physical anthropologist would posit the existence of a "Nordic" or "Alpine" race or subrace. But although

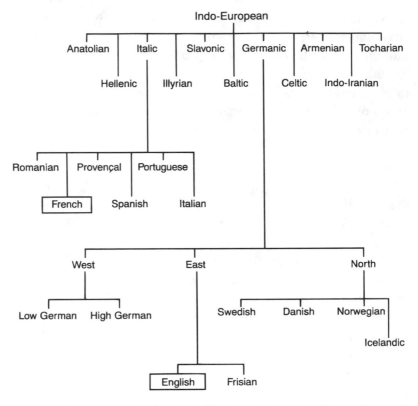

Fig. 25. Indo-European Origins of English and French. Adapted from diagrams in Renfrew, *Archaeology and Language*.

Hooton tries to preserve the "major" races as distinct lineages, his diagram at least implies that the lineages can rejoin. However, in the period following World War II physical anthropologists have generally tended toward an explanation of interpopulation biological variation in terms of differences in individual gene frequencies, rather than separately or semi-separately evolving lineages. The underlying model here would be continuous variation, along clines, rather than bifurcating "racial" groups—that is, intermediate groups can almost always be found between any pair of populations that are distant from each other. Perhaps there never really

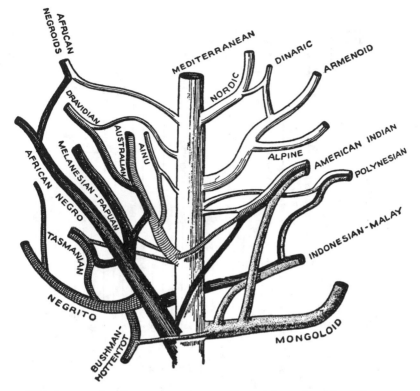

This is not a family tree, but a sort of arterial trunk with offshoots and connecting vessels.

Fig. 26. The blood streams of human races. Reprinted, by permission of the publisher, from *Up from the Ape* by Earnest A. Hooton (New York: Macmillan, 1932) 582.

were any completely separate lineages—perhaps the hypothesized bifurcations never occurred.

This issue, however, like most others in the human sciences, has never been completely settled. A recent attempt has been made, in fact, not only to describe subspecific biological variation in terms of racial lineages but also to link these lineages with linguistic diversification. Figure 27 is based on recent work by the population geneticist L. L. Cavalli-Sforza. Here a statistical

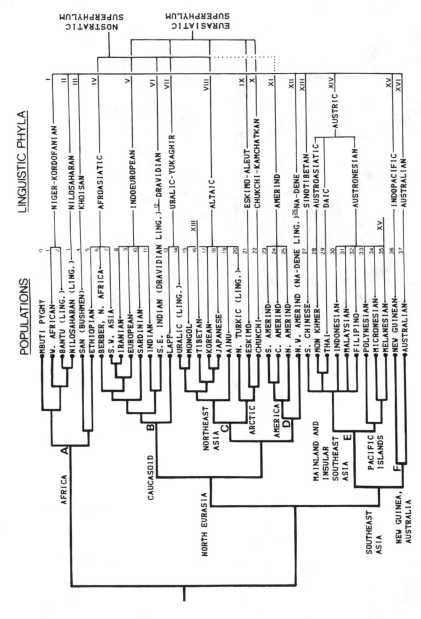

Fig. 27. Intersecting tree diagrams based on genetic and linguistic data according to Cavalli-Sforza. Reprinted, by permission of the University of Chicago Press, from R. Bateman, I. Goddard, R. O'Grady, V. A. Funk, R. Mooi, W. J. Kress, and P. Connell, "Speaking of Forked Tongues: The Feasibility of Reconciling Human Phylogeny and the History of Language," *Current Anthropology* 31, no. 1 (1990). © Wenner Gren Foundation for Anthropological Research.

method has been used to "fit" tree diagrams to gene frequency and historical linguistic data, and a high correlation has been found between the biological population tree and the historical linguistic tree.[10] This model is a return to the family tree with a vengeance. But we can accept this model only if we accept the underlying premise that human populations diverge in this manner. Seen another way, the data suggest the not terribly surprising conclusion that populations that are or were historically close geographically tend to be like each other genetically and to speak related languages.

Are there any overall themes that can be detected in the evolution of diversifying languages? Were similar paths taken by separate language groups, and if so, how could any such regularities be explained? Morris Swadesh, an anthropological linguist of the mid-twentieth century, developed a comprehensive model, based on historical linguistic principles, of regular processes at work in the evolution of languages (as distinct from language in general or its biological substrates). In Swadesh's scheme, the growth of languages has three stages: (1) local, (2) classic, and (3) world. These linguistic stages correspond to stages in the development of social complexity. With regard to the formation of modern world languages (e.g., English, French, Chinese), he writes:

1. Internal inflections formed by consonantal vowel alternations have been lost or reduced in number. New instances of internal inflections are few and limited in scope. The old ones are generally confined to traditional elements of the language; rarely are they applied to new loan words.
2. There are more instances in which inflective categories formed by affixation are reduced in number than cases in which new categories of this type have been added. Relational particles and auxiliary words sometimes fill the function of old inflective endings.[11]

Recall here our discussion in chapter 4 of the regular past tense in English. The irregular past tenses formed by internal inflection or gross changes in morphology are associated with the historically ancient core vocabulary of the language, whereas newly introduced verbs always take the regular past tense.

With respect to the development from local to classic languages, Swadesh makes these comments:

> The material we have surveyed . . . suggests that languages in the local stage had limited sets of phonemes available for lexical contrast, but complex patterns of alternates used in extensive paradigms of internal inflection; that the lexicon was small and the inflection complex; and that different languages were relatively similar with regard to all these features. The development since that time has been toward a greatly increased vocabulary with a more or less drastic reduction in inflection.[12]

All of these points would support the hypothesis that languages become, in Sapir's terms, more analytic as the societies of their users become more complex. With respect to the time line for human evolution, all human societies would have been at the local stage as recently as roughly five thousand years ago. In his introduction to Swadesh's book, the linguist Dell Hymes offers a "social ecological" explanation for this apparent relationship between linguistic and social development, along the lines that we have already considered:

> Differential complexity in surface word-structure may well be adaptive, complexity being a function of boundary maintenance in the case of small communities and groups, and simplicity a function of a language's use as a lingua franca.[13]

Now this does not suggest that in some simplistic way languages become more or less "complex" in some absolute sense during the course of evolution of the cultures with which they are associated. What is suggested is that as societies become more complex, they need larger lexicons, and that as lexicons increase, the morphological processes of word formation become simpler.

Students of linguistics will know that any such relationship between linguistic structure and societal complexity has been vehemently denied not only by the Chomskyan school but also by earlier structural and anthropological linguists, at least partly because of this idea's association with abandoned and sometimes racist theories about social evolution. Here, for example, is Charles Hockett writing on the subject in 1958:

> There is no discernible correlation between the placement of a language on the analytic-synthetic scale and anything else about either the language or other aspects of the life of its speakers. Some nineteenth century scholars proposed theories to the contrary, some of which have become part of the folklore about language current among educated laymen today.[14]

Otto Jespersen was one of those nineteenth-century scholars. While upholding the notion of a relationship between the development of social complexity and reduction in linguistic synthesis, he criticized the value-laden (perhaps racist) evolutionary schemas of earlier philologists.[15] Except insofar as Jespersen's theory has been taken as a universal statement and refuted with counterexamples, the principal theory—that various aspects of linguistic synthesis may be *related to,* that is correlated with, other aspects of social life—has apparently not been tested through the use of acceptable statistical procedures. Reluctance on the part of anthropologists and linguists to deal with questions such as this appears to have two sources. First, American anthropology following Boas rejected virtually all attempts to describe differences among languages and cultures in evolutionary terms. As already suggested the motive for this was a reaction against the racism that had pervaded anthropology prior to Boas. Second was the desire of Chomskyan linguists to support the notion of universality in linguistic structure.[16]

In the struggle against racist social theory, Chomskyan theory, in fact, and Chomsky personally, have appeared as champions. Dell Hymes notes with approval that Chomsky was probably more widely known for his political activism and his criticism of U.S. government policies during the 1960s and 1970s than for his revolutionary impact on linguistics. The following passage is from a review by Hymes of an intellectual biography of Chomsky:

> Chomsky's political role is advertised on the book jacket, sympathetically sketched in Lyons' introduction, and noted as not unconnected with his theory of language. It is not much analyzed, and the consideration is prefatory. The book ends on Chomsky's significance in linguistics alone. Now, having been in England at the time, I should like to enter an informed doubt that the more than a thousand who attended his lectures on language and mind in Oxford in the spring of 1969, or who filled the streets in London waiting for a lecture there, were moved by visions of a better base structure. Many of them came moved by the figure of a dramatically successful scholar who would put his mind and to some extent his body on the line for causes that matter—a man who publicly and commitedly broke with the age-old tradition of *trahison des clercs,* in which so many of us, recovered from our fright of the young in the '60's, are beginning to wallow again, rationalizing our toleration of the intolerable as defense of the academy of civility. Chomsky was a man who said simply that intellectuals should not lie, and more than that, a man who exposed some of the lies and liars.[17]

But with regard to the underlying ideological motive to deploy, as a defense against racism, principles of universality against the idea that languages and societies might evolve, it is ironic to note the liberal or even left-wing political credentials of both Swadesh and Hymes, as well as those of Chomsky. Swadesh was unable to find academic employment in the United States after running into political problems during the McCarthy era. In addition to recognizing the scholarly deficiencies of the universalist position, Hymes also describes its political deficiencies trenchantly:

> To say that every language has a sufficiently rich vocabulary for the expression of all the distinctions that are important in the society using it is to beg a host of questions; it is a form of "functionalist optimism" or Panglossia,[18] that would not pass muster for a moment in the political circles in which Chomsky figures, if seriously considered: cf. 'every society has sufficiently rich resources

for the satisfaction of all the needs that are important to it'; the general form of the proposition.[19]

What Swadesh and Hymes are doing, in fact, is simply drawing attention to regularities in the development of language and social life that need explanation.

If we are to accept these differences in languages and the social and technological complexity of the societies with which they are associated, how can we account for them? As was pointed out above, innovations in language, both signed and spoken, may have had one source or many. The usual way of tracing similarities in language that may result from common descent is according to a method now known as lexicostatistics, a method employed in less mathematical form by the philologists of the late eighteenth and early nineteenth centuries who first worked out the presumed interrelationships among Indo-European languages. This method proceeds through the collection of sound/meaning correspondences—that is, by the identification of lists of presumed cognates, in languages of varying degrees of assumed relationships. The rates at which the sounds related to various meanings seem to change over time are then estimated statistically based on historically known times of linguistic separation. For example, the time needed to accumulate the changes in sound/meaning correspondence between modern French and modern Italian is known from the historical record. Rates of change so estimated across a variety of languages can then be averaged and extended into the historically unknown past, assuming one believes that these rates are fairly constant and one accepts more or less the "tree" model of linguistic diversification. Clearly as this sort of analysis is extended further and further back in time, putative relationships among existing languages become murkier and murkier. Virtually all linguists accept, in general, the model of Indo-European diversification that has been presented here, but beyond that, other putative relationships, such as those supposedly linking Indo-European and what are now called Uralic (containing Hungarian, Finnish, etc.)

and Altaic (Turkish, Mongolian, etc.) into the so-called "Nostratic" family, are controversial. So, there would be widespread agreement on reconstruction back perhaps five thousand years to perhaps twenty or more possibly unrelated language families. Clearly to have an answer to the questions "one source or many?" and "when did it all start?" we would have to have much greater time depth than this.

If we examine what are supposed to be universals in languages and universal processes in language diversification and ask why these should exist, this book should have suggested that we are confronted with essentially three possible answers. First, absolute universals or universal tendencies could result simply from our genetic endowment—we might have no choice but to construct our languages as we do. Second, language (meaning spoken language) might have been invented, in its modern form, only once and spread from one source to all of the world's peoples. It would then have diversified according, perhaps, to structural rules inherent in language itself. Third, innovations in language might have arisen in a variety of locations over a long period of time. These innovations might have been shared by the peoples who invented them with their neighbors. Any particular innovation, relative pronouns for example, might have been invented independently in several locations. Regularities among languages would then be accounted for by biologically similar animals implementing and applying these innovations to similar problems in similar ways. The reader should by now have no doubt that this third possibility is the current author's preferred answer to the question.

Let us now return to a concrete example that we have been considering throughout this book in terms of semantic phonology. If it is true, as has been claimed, that all languages (including signed languages) have words that can be classified as either nouns or verbs, we can ask again whether this results from innate properties of the mind, or whether it results from invention. Our extended discussion of semantic phonology should serve to convince the reader that the most likely way for these categories to emerge is through processes of observation and interaction based on practical and significant human activities. Language is not the only realm of human activity in which obvious regularities have been observed. Anthropologists encountered numerous examples of similar patterns in cultural development, and early in the endeavor to describe the world's cultures these were ascribed to a so-called "psychic unity" of mankind, and later to "diffusion" from more to less advanced groups. Simply put, better explanations are now available in terms of similar cognitive capacities being applied to similar problems over extended periods of time, combined with information exchange among groups.

We could ask again, if language-aided thought is everywhere the same, why have some peoples developed more complex technologies and social structures than some others? As we have seen anthropologists have avoided this issue because of the association of answers to this question with racist ideology, sometimes termed "Social Darwinism." As a simple way to guard against racist interpretations of our common history as a species, we should keep in mind how recent any of these differences in complexity are. All human beings who were alive on Earth up until about ten thousand years ago lived at roughly the same, relatively low level of complexity—thus, for more than 99% of our time on Earth we all pursued roughly the same way of life. What would our Martian anthropologist have predicted for any of us ten thousand years ago? The similarities among people, the technologically complex and the technologically simple, deaf people and hearing, vastly outweigh the differences. The importance of studying the differences is to gain new insight into the nature of the human condition generally, but any responsible theorist must be aware of the unsavory history of this sort of speculation. These differences can, in general, be accounted for in terms of differences in population density and pressure, access to natural resources, ideology, and geographic location at the center or the periphery of major land masses. For most of our history as human beings, however, we have all lived at a very simple technological level, and there is no assurance that we will not all return to that level.

It is by now almost trite to point out that our modern civilization, supported by energy conversion on a scale hitherto unknown, may not be sustainable. If history and archaeology teach us nothing else, it is that within the short span of time during which human beings have created civilizations, these have come and gone with surprising regularity. The ruins left by formerly mighty peoples litter every continent except remote Australia. Organizations with staying power have recognized explicitly the transitory nature of human institutions. The well-known Latin phrase "*sic transit gloria mundi*" is spoken at the enthronement of new popes to remind them of the complacency and arrogance that follow presumptions of permanence and to remind them of the greater glory of the world to come. A similar phrase is said to have been spoken to generals of the Roman republic when their victories were being celebrated with a triumph. Unlike many other native American civilizations, that of the Maya may not have been a victim of outside invaders—instead it seems to have imploded or collapsed under its own weight. So complete was its self-destruction that the Mayan people themselves, who live in contemporary times in the rain forests of the Yucatan peninsula and the highlands of Guatemala, forgot where the ruins of many of their cities were located, and forgot even how to read the exquisite script in which their ancestors had written their language. The script has been largely deciphered by scholars from an alien culture, but this was possible only because the people themselves, and their language, had survived the death of the civilization.

So this book ends with a plea. Not a plea to save the world, which would exceed the scope of this book, but a plea for a return to a more unified science of language and, more broadly, of the human condition. In this book we have explored to a limited extent some of the divisions within the discipline of linguistics, divisions that concern the very nature of the discipline's subject matter. Writing in 1998, Mark Turner, a cognitive scientist at the University of Maryland, made the following comment about the consequences of this state of affairs: "Two linguists of the greatest eminence and learning can disagree about fundamental questions (does syntax depend on meaning?) without submitting to a generally respected method for deciding which, if either, of them is right. The best hope for springing linguistics from this disciplinary bind lies in bringing to bear other human sciences such as anthropology, cognitive science, and neuroscience."[20] But things are not all that much better in anthropology.

In 1998 the physical anthropologist Matt Cartmill commented on the assault being mounted against Darwinian theory by both fundamentalist religious groups on the right and radical social scientists, notably anthropologists, on the left, in the latter case under the guise of postmodernism. Religious people have always felt threatened by Darwinian theory for reasons that were introduced at the beginning of this book, especially its apparent purposelessness, although some organized religions have found ways to accommodate their religious views of creation with the evolutionary theory of Darwin. Cartmill sums up the opposition of left-wing groups to Darwinism in this trenchant sentence: "Anyone who claims to have objective knowledge about anything is trying to control and dominate the rest of us."[21] Darwinian theory also has an unhealthy past with respect to its use in the justification of exploitative socioeconomic policies (Social Darwinism) and its apparent glorification of competition. Instead of railing against these criticisms, Cartmill takes an unusual tack for a biologically oriented scholar and calls instead for a degree of reconciliation. His conclusions provide a perfect ending for this book:

> The broad outlines of the story of human evolution are known beyond a reasonable doubt. However, science hasn't yet found satisfying, law-based natural explanations for most of the details of that story. All that we scientists can do is admit our ignorance and keep looking. Our ignorance doesn't prove anything one way or the other about divine plans or purposes behind the flow of his-

tory. Anybody who says it does is pushing a religious doctrine. Both the religious creationists of the right and the secular creationists of the left object and say that a lot of evolutionists are doing just that in the name of science—and to this extent they are unfortunately right. . . . Humility isn't just a cardinal virtue in Christian doctrine; it's also a virtue in the practice of science.[22]

This observation becomes all the more pertinent when the science in question is that of the human condition.

Notes

The chapter title is taken from the title of an article by Bateman et al. (1990). Jerry Gill uses this phrase, in the sense of prevarication, in the title of one of the chapters in his book *If a chimpanzee could talk* (1997).

1. Genesis 11.1–10.
2. Judges 12.1–6.
3. In the Lerner and Loewe musical, *My Fair Lady*.
4. Wilcox (1984).
5. Markowicz and Woodward (1975).
6. For example, Davidson and Noble (1989).
7. For example, "These are the sons of Ham, after their families, after their tongues, and in their nations." Genesis 10.20.
8. See, for example, Dixon (1997, 52–53). The tree diagram for English and French presented here is based upon separate diagrams in Renfrew (1989), but in his book published in 1971, Swadesh pointed out that the tree diagram was not always the best way to present data on linguistic divergence. He preferred instead "*a chain, mesh, or net*" (Swadesh 1971, 33).
9. Hooton (1932).
10. Cavalli-Sforza et al. (1988). See also Bateman et al. (1990) and Cavalli-Sforza and Cavalli-Sforza (1995, 190) for discussion of non-tree approaches to linguistic diversification.
11. Swadesh (1971, 76).
12. Ibid. 112f).
13. Hymes (1971, vii).
14. Hockett (1958, 181).
15. Jespersen (1894).
16. Study of the evolution of grammatical processes, or grammaticization, has began to reemerge in standard linguistics (see Bybee, 1998).
17. Hymes (1974, 329).

18. After Doctor Pangloss, the character in Voltaire's *Candide* whose constant refrain was Leibniz's credo of optimism: "All is for the best in this best of all possible worlds."

19. Hymes (1974, 317).

20. Turner (1998, 73). Quoted with permission of the author.

21. Cartmill (1998, 80).

22. Ibid. (83).

Bibliography

Armstrong, D. F. 1983. Iconicity, arbitrariness, and duality of patterning in signed and spoken language: Perspectives on language evolution. *Sign Language Studies* 38:51–69.

———. 1987. Word, sign, and object. *Journal of the Washington Academy of Sciences* 77 (1): 26–31.

Armstrong, D. F., W. C. Stokoe, and S. E. Wilcox. 1995. *Gesture and the nature of language.* Cambridge: Cambridge University Press.

Bateman, R., I. Goddard, R. O'Grady, V. A. Funk, R. Mooi, W. J. Kress, and P. Cannell. 1990. Speaking of forked tongues: The feasibility of reconciling human phylogeny and the history of language. *Current Anthropology* 31 (1): 1–24.

Baynton, D. C. 1996. *Forbidden signs: American culture and the campaign against sign language.* Chicago: University of Chicago Press.

Beakan, M. 1996. *The making of language.* Edinburgh: Edinburgh University Press.

Begun, D. R. 1994. Relations among the great apes and humans: New interpretations based on the fossil record. *Yearbook of Physical Anthropology* 37:11–63.

Bernstein, B. 1964. Aspects of language and learning in the social process. In *Language in culture and society,* edited by D. Hymes, 251–63. New York: Harper and Row.

Bickerton, D. 1990. *Language and species.* Chicago: University of Chicago Press.

Bishop, D. V. M. 1997. Editorial: A gene for grammar? *Semiotic Review of Books* 7 (2): 1–2.

Boas, F. [1911] 1963. *The mind of primitive man.* Reprint, New York: Free Press.

Bogen, J. 1973. The other side of the brain: An appositional mind. In *The nature of human consciousness,* edited by R. E. Ornstein, 101–25. New York: Viking Press.

Bonvillian, J. D., and H. C. Richards. 1993. The development of hand preference in children's early signing. *Sign Language Studies* 78:1–14.

Branson, J., D. Miller, and I. G. Marsaja. 1996. Everyone here speaks sign language, too: A deaf village in Bali, Indonesia. In *Multicultural aspects of sociolinguistics in deaf communities,* edited by C. Lucas, 39–57. Washington, D.C.: Gallaudet University Press.

Brasington, D. 1994. Distinctive features. In *The Encyclopedia of Languages and Linguistics,* edited by R. E. Asher, 2:1042–50. Oxford: Pergamon Press.

Brownell, H. H., D. Michell, J. Powelson, and H. Gardner. 1983. Surprise but not coherence: Sensitivity to verbal humor in right-hemisphere patients. *Brain and Language* 18:20–27.

Buchler, J., ed. 1955. *Philosophical writings of Peirce.* New York: Dover Publications.

Buettner-Janusch, J. 1966. *Origins of man.* New York: John Wiley and Sons.

Bybee, J. 1998. The evolution of grammar. Paper presented at the annual meeting of the American Association for the Advancement of Science, Philadelphia.

Cartmill, M. 1998. Oppressed by evolution. *Discover* 19 (3): 78–83.

Cavalli-Sforza, L. L., A. Piazza, P. Menozzi, and J. Mountain. 1988. Reconstruction of human evolution: Bringing together genetic, archaeological, and linguistic data. *Proceedings of the National Academy of Sciences of the USA* 85:6002–6.

Cavalli-Sforza, L. L., and F. Cavalli-Sforza. 1995. *The great human diasporas.* Reading, Mass.: Addison-Wesley.

Chomsky, N. 1957. *Syntactic structures.* The Hague: Mouton.

———. 1965. *Aspects of the theory of syntax.* Cambridge, Mass.: MIT Press.

———. 1966. *Cartesian linguistics.* New York: Harper and Row.

———. 1995. *The minimalist program.* Cambridge, Mass.: MIT Press.

Coe, M. D. 1992. *Breaking the Maya code.* London: Thames and Hudson.

Cook, V. 1988. *Chomsky's universal grammar.* Oxford: Basil Blackwell.

Corballis, M. C. 1991. *The lopsided ape: Evolution of the generative mind.* Oxford: Oxford University Press.

Darwin, C. [1845] 1937. *The voyage of the Beagle.* Reprint, New York: P. F. Collier and Son.

———. [1859] 1958. *The origin of species.* Reprint, New York: New American Library.

Davidson, I., and W. Noble. 1989. The archaeology of perception: Traces of depiction and language. *Current Anthropology* 30(2):124–55.

Deacon, T. W. 1997. *The symbolic species: The co-evolution of language and the brain.* New York: W. W. Norton.

Deuchar, M. 1983. Implications of sign language research for linguistic theory. In *Proceedings of the III International Symposium on Sign Language Research,* edited by W. C. Stokoe and V. Volterra. Silver Spring, Md.: Linstok Press.

Diamond, J. 1992. *The third chimpanzee.* New York: HarperCollins.

Dimond, S. 1972. *The double brain.* Baltimore: Williams and Wilkins.

Dixon, R. M. W. 1997. *The rise and fall of languages.* Cambridge: Cambridge University Press.

Donald, M. 1991. *Origins of the modern mind.* Cambridge, Mass.: Harvard University Press.

Eastman, G. 1989. *From mime to sign.* Silver Spring, Md.: TJ Publishers.

Edwards, B. 1989. *Drawing on the right side of the brain.* New York: Putnam.

Eisenson, J. 1962. Language and intellectual modifications associated with right cerebral damage. *Language and Speech* 5:49–53.

Farnell, B. 1995. *Do you see what I mean? Plains Indian sign talk and the embodiment of action.* Austin: University of Texas Press.

Fisher, S. E., F. Vargha-Khadem, K. E. Watkins, A. P. Monaco, and M. E. Pembrey. 1998. Localisation of a gene implicated in severe speech and language disorder. *Nature Genetics* 18(2):168–70.

Fouts, R., and S. T. Mills. 1997. *Next of kin.* New York: William Morrow.

Frishberg, N. 1975. Arbitrariness and iconicity: Historical change in American Sign Language. *Language* 51:699–719.

Gallaudet, E.M. 1983. *History of the college for the deaf, 1857-1907.* Washington, D.C.: Gallaudet College Press.

Gannon, P. J., R. L. Holloway, D. C. Broadfield, and A. R. Braun. 1998. Asymmetry of chimpanzee planum temporale: Humanlike brain pattern of Wernicke's area homolog. *Science* 279 (5348):220–22.

Gibson, K. 1997. Review of *The wisdom of the bones* by Alan Walker and Pat Shipman. *Evolution of Communication* 1 (1): 153-155.

Gill, J. H. 1997. *If a chimpanzee could talk and other reflections on language acquisition.* Tucson: University of Arizona Press.

Goffman, E. 1971. *Relations in public.* New York: Harper and Row.

Gopnick, M. 1990. Feature-blind grammar and dysphasia. *Nature* 344:715.

Gould, S. J., and R. C. Lewontin. 1979. The spandrels of San Marco and the Panglossian program: A critique of the adaptationist programme. *Proceedings of the Royal Society of London* 205:281–88.

Greenberg, J. H. 1968. *Anthropological linguistics.* New York: Random House.

Groce, N. E. 1985. *Everyone here spoke sign language: Hereditary deafness on Martha's Vineyard.* Cambridge, Mass.: Harvard University Press.

Harris, R. A. 1993. *The linguistics wars.* Oxford: Oxford University Press.

Hertz, R. 1909. The pre-eminence of the right hand: A study in religious polarity. Translated by R. Needham. In *Right and left,* edited by R. Needham. Chicago: University of Chicago Press.

Hewes, G. W. 1976. The current status of the gestural theory of language origin. In *Origins and evolution of language and speech,* edited by S. R. Harnad, H. D. Steklis, and J. Lancaster. *Annals of the New York Academy of Sciences* 280:482–504.

———. 1983. Comment on iconicity, arbitrariness, and duality. *Sign Language Studies* 38:70–75.

Hockett, C. 1958. *A course in modern linguistics.* New York: Macmillan.

———. 1978. In search of Jove's brow. *American Speech* 53 (4):242–313.

Hollander, J. 1974. Coiled Alizarine. In *On Noam Chomsky: Critical essays,* edited by G. Harman (New York: Anchor Books). First published in *The night mirror* (New York: Atheneum, 1971).

Howell, F. C. 1965. *Early man.* New York: Time-Life Books.

Hooton, E. A. 1932. *Up from the ape.* New York: Macmillan.

Huneker, J. 1919. *The poems and prose poems of Charles Baudelaire.* New York: Brentano's.

Hymes, D. 1971. Foreword to *The origin and diversification of language,* by M. Swadesh. Chicago: Aldine.

———. 1973. On the origins and foundations of inequality among speakers. *Dædalus* (summer): 59–68.

———. 1974. Review of *Noam Chomsky.* In *On Noam Chomsky: Critical essays,* edited by G. Harman (New York: Anchor Books). First published in *Language* 48 (1972): 416–27.

Jakobson, R. 1956. Two aspects of language and two types of aphasic disturbances. In *Fundamentals of language,* edited by R. Jakobson and M. Halle. The Hague: Mouton.

James, W. [1890] 1983. *The principles of psychology.* Reprint, Cambridge, Mass.: Harvard University Press.

Jespersen, O. 1894. *Progress in language.* New York: Macmillan.

Johnson, R. E. 1991. Sign language, culture, and community in a traditional Yucatec Maya village. *Sign Language Studies* 73:461–74.

Johnson, R. E., S. K. Liddell, and C. Erting. 1989. *Unlocking the curriculum: Principles for achieving success in deaf education.* GRI Working Paper Series, no. 89-3. Washington, D.C.: Gallaudet University Research Institute.

Kendon, A. 1989. *Sign Languages of aboriginal Austrailia.* Cambridge: Cambridge University Press.

———. 1997. An agenda for gesture studies. *Semiotic Review of Books* 7 (2): 8–12.

Kimura, D. 1976. The neural basis of language *qua* gesture. In *Studies in neurolinguistics,* vol. 2, edited by H. Whitaker and H. A. Whitaker. New York: Academic Press.

———. 1981. Neural mechanisms in manual signing. *Sign Language Studies* 33:291–312.

———. 1993. *Neuromotor mechanisms in human communication.* Oxford: Oxford University Press.

King, B. J. 1994. *The information continuum: Evolution of social information transfer in monkeys, apes, and hominids.* Santa Fe: School of American Research Press.

King, B. J., and S. Shanker. 1997. The expulsion of the primates from the garden of language. *Evolution of Communication* 1(1): 59–99.

Kipling, R. [1902] 1992. *Just so stories.* Reprint, New York: Alfred A. Knopf.

Kluckhohn, C., and D. Leighton. 1951. *The Navaho.* Cambridge, Mass.: Harvard University Press.

Kroeber, T. 1963. *Ishi in two worlds.* Berkeley: University of California Press.

Kuhl, P. K., K. A. Williams, F. Lacerda, K. N. Stevens, and B. Lindblom. 1992. Linguistic experience alters phonetic perception in infants by 6 months of age. *Science* 255:606–8.

Kuhn, T. S. 1962. *The structure of scientific revolutions.* Chicago: University of Chicago Press.

Laughlin, C. D., and E. G. D'Aquili. 1974. *Biogenetic structuralism.* New York: Columbia University Press.

Leavens, D. A., W. D. Hopkins, and K. A. Bard. 1996. Indexical and referential pointing in chimpanzees (Pan troglodytes). *Journal of Comparative Psychology* 110:346–53.

Leach, E. 1970. *Claude Lévi-Strauss.* New York: Viking.

Lees, R. B. 1974. Review of *Syntactic structures*. In *On Noam Chomsky: Critical essays,* edited by G. Harman (New York: Anchor Books). First published in *Language* 33 (1957): 375–405.

Le Gros Clark, W. E. 1963. *The antecedents of man.* Edinburgh: Edinburgh University Press, 1959. Reprint, New York: Harper and Row.

Lévi-Strauss, C. 1962. *La pensée sauvage.* Paris: Plon.

Liddell, S. 1996. Spatial representations in discourse: Comparing spoken and signed language. *Lingua* 98:145–67.

Lieberman, P. 1991. *Uniquely human.* Cambridge, Mass.: Harvard University Press.

Lucy, J. A. 1992. *Grammatical categories and cognition: A case study of the linguistic relativity hypothesis.* Cambridge: Cambridge University Press.

Markowicz, H., and J. Woodward. 1975. *Language and the maintenance of ethnic boundaries in the deaf community.* Paper presented at the Conference on Culture and Communication, Temple University, Philadelphia. Reprinted in *How you gonna get to heaven if you can't talk to Jesus,* edited by J. Woodward. Silver Spring, Md.: TJ Publishers, 1982.

McNeill, D. 1992. *Hand and mind: What gestures reveal about thought.* Chicago: University of Chicago Press.

McNeill, D., and P. Freiberger. 1993. *Fuzzy logic.* New York: Simon and Schuster.

Messing, L. 1994. Bimodal communication: Signing skill and tenseness. *Sign Language Studies* 84:209–20.

Miller, G. A. 1991. *The science of words.* New York: Scientific American Library.

Mills, C. B., and I. K. Jordan. 1980. Timing sensitivity and age as predictors of sign language learning. *Sign Language Studies* 26:15–28.

Mirzoeff, N. 1995. *Silent poetry: Deafness, sign, and visual culture in modern France.* Princeton: Princeton University Press.

Myklebust, H. 1957. *The psychology of deafness.* New York: Grune and Stratton.

Napier, J. R. 1970. *The roots of mankind.* Washington, D.C.: Smithsonian Institution Press.

Napier, J. R., and P. H. Napier. 1967. *A handbook of living primates.* New York: Academic Press.

Neisser, A. 1983. *The other side of silence.* New York: Knopf.

Newcombe, F., R. Oldfield, and A. Wingfield. 1965. Object naming by dysphasic patients. *Nature* 207:1217–18.

Padden, C. 1990. Rethinking fingerspelling. *Signpost* (October): 2–4.

Padden, C., and T. Humphries. 1988. *Deaf in America: Voices from a culture.* Cambridge, Mass.: Harvard University Press.

Perrett, D. I., M. H. Harries, R. Bevan, S. Thomas, P. J. Benson, A. J. Mistlin, A. J. Chitty, J. K. Hietanen, and J. E. Ortega. 1989. Frameworks of analysis for neural representation of animate objects and actions. *Journal of Experimental Biology* 146:87–113.

Perrett, D. I., A. J. Mistlin, and A. J. Chitty. 1987. Visual cells responsive to faces. *Trends in Neuroscience* 10:358–64.

Peters, M. 1990. Interaction of vocal and manual movements. In *Cerebral control of speech and limb movements,* edited by G. R. Hammond, 535–74. Amsterdam: North Holland.

Pike, K. 1964. Towards a theory of the structure of human behavior. In *Language in culture and society,* edited by D. Hymes. New York: Harper and Row.

Pinker, S. 1991. Rules of language. *Science* 253:530–35.

———. 1994. *The language instinct.* New York: William Morrow.

Poizner, H., and H. Lane. 1979. Cerebral asymmetry in the perception of American Sign Language. *Brain and Language* 7: 210-226.

Premack, D. 1986. *Gavagai! Or the future history of the animal language controversy.* Cambridge, Mass.: MIT Press.

Pulleyblank, E. G. 1986. The meaning of duality of patterning and its importance in language evolution. *Sign Language Studies* 51:101–20.

Quine, W. V. 1953. *From a logical point of view.* Cambridge, Mass.: Harvard University Press.

———. 1960. *Word and object.* Cambridge, Mass.: MIT Press.

———. 1974. Methodological reflections on current linguistic theory. In *On Noam Chomsky: Critical essays,* edited by G. Harman. New York: Anchor Books.

Renfrew, C. 1987. *Archaeology and language.* Cambridge: Cambridge University Press.

Richman, B. 1997. Common fallacies that plague most language origins stories. *LOS Forum,* no. 24:15–39.

Sacks, O. W. 1995. *An anthropologist on Mars.* New York: Knopf.

Sapir, E. 1921. *Language.* New York: Harcourt, Brace, and World.

———. 1964. Conceptual categories in primitive languages. In *Language in culture and society,* edited by D. Hymes (New York: Harper and Row). First published in *Science* 74 (1931):578.

Sarles, H. D. 1974. Could a non h? In *Language origins,* edited by R. W. Wescott, G. W. Hewes, and W. C. Stokoe, 218–38. Silver Spring, Md.: Linstok Press.

Savage-Rumbaugh, E. S., and R. Lewin. 1994. *Kanzi: The ape at the brink of the human mind.* New York: John Wiley.

Schulte, J. 1992. *Wittgenstein.* Albany: State University of New York Press.

Shattuck, R. 1985. Words and images: Thinking and translation. *Dædalus* 114(4): 201–14.

Smith, J. M., and E. Szathmáry. 1995. *The major transitions in evolution.* New York: WH Freeman.

Söderfeldt, B., J. Rönnberg, and J. Risberg. 1994. Regional cerebral blood flow during sign language perception: Deaf and hearing subjects with deaf parents compared. *Sign Language Studies* 84:199–208.

Spence, J. *The memory palace of Matteo Ricci.* New York: Penguin Books.

Stewart, A. H. 1976. *Graphic representation of models in linguistic theory.* Bloomington: Indiana University Press.

Stokoe, W. C. 1960. *Sign language structure: An outline of the visual communication systems of the American deaf. Studies in Linguistics: Occasional Papers 8.* Buffalo: University of Buffalo Department of Anthropology and Linguistics.

———. 1980. Sign language structure. *Annual Review of Anthropology* 9:365–90.

———. 1991. Semantic phonology. *Sign Language Studies* 71:107–14.

Stokoe, W. C., D. C. Casterline, and C. G. Croneberg. 1965. *A dictionary of American Sign Language on linguistic principles.* Washington, D.C.: Gallaudet College Press.

Supalla, T., and E. Newport. 1978. How many seats in a chair? The derivation of nouns and verbs in American Sign Language. In *Understanding language through sign language research,* edited by P. Siple. New York: Academic Press.

Swadesh, M. 1971. *The origin and diversification of language.* Chicago: Aldine.

Tattersall, I. 1995. *The fossil trail.* Oxford: Oxford University Press.

Teilhard de Chardin, P. 1961. *The phenomenon of man.* New York: Harper and Row, 1959. Reprint, New York: Harper Torchbooks.

Tillman, F. A., B. Berofsky, and J. O'Connor, eds. 1967. *Introductory philosophy.* New York: Harper and Row.

Truex, R. C., and M. B. Carpenter. 1969. *Human neuroanatomy.* 6th ed. Baltimore: Williams and Wilkins.

Turner, M. 1998. Poetry for the newborn brain. *Bostonia* (spring): 72–73.

Turner, V. 1967. *The forest of symbols.* Ithaca, N.Y.: Cornell University Press.

Tylor, E. B. [1881] 1965. *Anthropology.* Reprint, Ann Arbor: University of Michigan Press.

Umiker-Sebeok, D., and T. Sebeok. 1978. *Aboriginal sign languages of the Americas and Australia.* New York: Plenum Press.

van Marle, J. 1994. Paradigms. In *The Encyclopedia of Languages and Linguistics,* edited by R. E. Asher, 6:2927–30. Oxford: Pergamon Press.

Wapner, W., H. Hamby, and H. Gardner. 1981. The role of the right hemisphere in apprehension of complex linguistic materials. *Brain and Language* 14:15–33.

Wescott, R. W., G. W. Hewes, and W. C. Stokoe. 1974. *Language origins.* Silver Spring, Md.: Linstok Press.

Whorf, B. L. 1956. *Language, thought, and reality; Selected writings.* Edited by J. B. Carroll. Cambridge, Mass.: MIT Press.

Wilcox, S. E. 1984. Stuck in school: A study of semantics and culture in a deaf education class. *Sign Language Studies* 43:141–64.

———. 1996. Hands and bodies, minds and souls: Or, how a sign linguist learned to stop worrying and love gesture. Paper presented at the Workshop on Integrating Language and Gesture, University of Delaware, Newark.

Winefield, R. 1987. *Never the twain shall meet: Bell, Gallaudet, and the communications debate.* Washington, D.C.: Gallaudet University Press.

Winner, E., and H. Gardner. 1977. The comprehension of metaphor in brain-damaged patients. *Brain* 100:717–29.

Wittgenstein, L. [1921] 1974. *Tractatus logico-philosophicus.* Translated from the German by D. F. Pears and B. F. McGuinness. Reprint, London: Routledge.

Index

Numbers in boldface refer to illustrations